Contents

Our change of name

Starting with this issue, *Focus on Gender* changes its name to *Gender and Development*. I would like to take the opportunity of welcoming all readers, new and established, to the journal.

In the two years since its inception, Oxfam's gender and development journal — the only one published in Britain which focuses primarily on these issues — has pursued a unique commitment: to offer a forum for discussion of gender and development issues to the widest possible audience, fusing the experience and research of development practice as well as academia. It is Oxfam's belief that this cross-fertilisation is of worth and interest to both major constituencies in our target readership.

Our intention is to make *Gender and Development* accessible to the widest possible readership, but this does not mean that we sacrifice the standard of the material that you read in the journal. Rather, it means following a policy of using clear, accessible language to express complex ideas. In this way, we hope to encourage contributions and readership among people who may not have had access to formal education, in South and North. Ultimately, this policy signifies Oxfam's commitment to ending the bias which has existed in development studies, of expressing ideas about the South in language accessible only to those who have had education from the North. For Guidelines for Contributors, write to me, at the Oxfam address.

To consolidate our commitment to provide a forum for the South as well as the North, practitioners as well as academics, *Gender and Development* has appointed an international Editorial Board (see inside back cover). Composed of academics, development practitioners, and activists within the women's movement, the Board will advise on the direction and editorial policy of the journal, identify themes for coverage, and will provide a refereeing function for articles, when appropriate.

Finally, from this issue, subscribers to the journal will find that they have been sent a copy of *Links*, the newsletter of Oxfam's Gender Team. Readers' comments and criticism of the journal, or *Links*, are welcomed and will find a forum in *Links*.

Caroline Sweetman

Editorial

This issue of *Gender and Development* examines the implications of the issue of culture, for gender and development work. Our culture is what determines the meaning that we attribute to every part of our existence. As such, awareness of the power of culture is of profound importance in understanding not only ourselves and other people, but gender relations, and even the notion of 'development' itself.

Culture determines power relations within society, influencing women's and men's access to and control over economic resources, and their ability to take decisions in the family and community. Economic and political forces both shape and are shaped by culture. 'Material processes – like the economy or politics – depend on "meaning" for their effects, and have cultural or ideological conditions of existence' (Hall 1992).

We need to acknowledge the extent to which our own attitudes are influenced by our cultural background. All human beings are products of a process of socialisation, which leads us to consider some aspects of our lives as natural and 'given'. Depending on who we are, where we come from, and our formative experiences, we attach different significance to particular things: the wearing of a head-dress, attendance at a funeral, walking on a public road. Different cultural biases colour every part of human existence, and affect the views and actions of individuals, organisations, and nations.

The concept of development is laden with the cultural values of post-colonialism, of Northern countries, and of economists. Over the last 30 years, development has been synonymous with a Northern-based notion of 'modernisation' – economic progress from a 'traditional' to a 'modern' society. Therefore when we consider the issue of culture this involves us in questioning assumptions about the sort of development which is currently being promoted, and the vision of the world which motivates it.

Modernisers have sought to export Northern social structures to the South, including the nuclear family, the secular State, and the ideal of female domesticity (Kabeer 1994). Development initiatives have thus profoundly changed social structures and social relations, including those between the sexes. As Sara Longwe observes in her article, 'a developmental intervention cannot leave traditional social practice untouched, nor ignore the existence of customary practice which stands in the way of development.'

Gender, culture, and tradition

Though the manner in which women's subordination is expressed differs from culture to culture, 'the secondary status of women is one of the true universals, a true pan-cultural fact' (Ortner 1974, quoted in O'Connell 1994, 88). Biological differences between women and men (sex) are overlaid with cultural notions about difference, which have no basis in biology (gender). Only when a woman is bearing and suckling a baby does nature place practical constraints on her behaviour: yet, throughout the world, biology is used as a rationale for women's subordination to men.

Different constraints on women exist from society to society, yet in each location, at any particular time, ideas of correct female behaviour are viewed as universal and unchanging. Gender ideology is embedded in notions of 'custom' and 'tradition' which direct women's and men's lives, and ensure conformity to the norms of society. By appealing to 'tradition', cultural practices which reinforce the power of men in our societies are venerated unquestioningly; but 'tradition is not the whole of the past but only a part of it consisting of "frozen movement", the result of deliberate choices endorsed by subsequent generations over a relatively long period' (UNESCO undated, 58).

However ancient and time-honoured they may seem, traditions may actually undergo alteration to suit changed economic, political, and social circumstances. What does not change is the underlying ideology of female inferiority, which is disguised in an idealised image of woman as perfect wife and mother.

This notion of the ideal woman rests on the need, within a patriarchal society, to enforce women's chastity outside marriage, and fidelity within it, since paternity is the ultimate definer of the identity of children. Women's modesty and sexual continence is thus critical to the survival of the family. In turn, women, as primary carers for their children, have responsibility for passing on societal values to their children. For these reasons, women are seen by societies across the world as guardians of culture.

Feminists in South and North reject both the idea of female inferiority and the unattainable ideal of perfect domesticity, which disguises women's subordination to male family members: 'we reject pedestals, queenhood and walking ten paces behind. To be recognised as human, levelly human, is enough' (Combahee River Collective, India).

JOHN OGLE/OXFAM

Teaching traditional songs and dances, in Tamil Nadu. In many societies, women are seen as the guardians and transmitters of culture, because of their responsibilities for the care of children.

Wife abuse: enforcing conformity

Women who challenge notions of female inferiority risk being ostracised by their communities, since such subordination goes unquestioned by the majority of men, as well as by many women. In her article, Maitrayee Mukhopadhyay explores the origins of the hostility that she encountered from South Asian men when she gave a talk about her experiences and work. While she was criticising sexism in South Asian society from the point of view of an 'insider', the problems of addressing culture as a development issue become still more complex if 'outsiders' are involved.

As Colletah Chitsike observes in her article, in reality women can, and do, hold positions of power and responsibility; yet these do not become recognised as 'traditional'. A woman who defies gender norms threatens the stability of the wider society. Women's achievements may be ignored, or, in extreme circumstances, women who violate cultural norms may be accused of witchcraft. 'Witchcraft is a way of dealing with women's power and its challenges, both within and without, and witchcraft accusation exposes the ambiguities and uncertainties created in the process of social change' (Amoah 1987).

The ultimate method of enforcing women's conformity to their traditional role is physical and mental violence, including rape. In some countries, forced sex within marriage has recently been recognised in law as rape. Both rape and wife beating are accepted as the norm in many cultures (Levinson, 1989).

In 1994, after years of lobbying from feminist organisations, the United Nations recognised violence against women to be a violation of human rights. Despite this belated recognition of one of the most widespread forms of abuse worldwide, development projects which address violence as an issue still encounter considerable resistance from national governments, international funders, and male community members. Although the law can play a leading role in condemning such practices through criminalising them, cultural norms must also change if abuse of women is to be eradicated.

In her article on Zimbabwe's Musasa Project, Sheelagh Stewart discusses the difficulties of working on a project which addresses the 'cultural issue' of violence against women. Those working to 'fight those aspects of our culture which betray us' (Moraga 1988) need allies to further the struggle. In the case of the Musasa Project, this meant working with decision makers and law enforcers, to educate men about women's right to live without the fear of male violence, and to enable women to use legal structures to ensure this.

Gender, culture, and crisis

Increased violence against women is an integral aspect of warfare. Just as a woman may be viewed as her husband's property, and rape in marriage as a way to assert this, in conflict she may be raped by other men as a means of violating her husband's rights over her. Jovanka Stojsavljevic, who works for Oxfam in Croatia, discusses the widespread sexual violence against women in the conflict in former Yugoslavia.

Whether the identity of a community is defined by ethnicity, religion or political belief, this identity becomes supremely important in such a time of crisis. In this light, forced impregnation of 'enemy' women may be seen as a deliberate attempt to colonise the enemy's territory by forcing women to give birth to babies who have the nationality of the rapist. As Jovanka Stojsavljevic observes, communities may disown and repudiate women who have been raped, because they have 'betrayed' their culture and violated the ideals of chastity.

Ironically, the attempts of feminists to publicise the hideous violence against women that has occurred during the conflict has been used by the warring sides themselves as a form of propaganda, to justify the political agenda of the nationalists. Jovanka Stojsavljevic discusses how feminist organisations in former Yugoslavia have resisted such incitements to involvement in conflict justified by ethnic or religious identity.

In her article, Sue Katz of Women Against Fundamentalism (WAF) promotes the ideal of the secular state, arguing that when religion becomes a part of national identity, religious and ethnic minorities are seen as 'alien', resulting in institutionalised racism. There is a need for clarity about the relationship which exists between religion and the growing 'fundamentalist' movement throughout the world. WAF provide a useful definition of fundamentalism: 'modern political movements which use religion as a basis for their attempt to win or consolidate power and extend social control' (WAF publicity 1994).

In its article, Women Living Under Muslim Laws (WLUML), an international organisation supporting women in Muslim countries, points out that religious fundamentalists appeal to unchanging tradition to promote the idea of a single, uniform Muslim world, which is by definition united in opposition to those of other faiths. In fact, there are great differences of belief and practice among Muslim individuals, families, and communities. A myth of an idealised Muslim woman, at the heart of a perfect family, justifies women's subordination to men, in fundamentalist interpretations of Islam.

While Islamic fundamentalism attracts much adverse publicity, particularly in Northern countries which have a predominantly Christian heritage, fundamentalist movements exist within other religions, including Christianity itself (Armstrong 1986). WAF's definition is broad enough to include a secular version of fundamentalism; there are marked similarities between the manipulation of religious texts by fundamentalists to justify women's subordination, and calls from Northern politicians for a return to the 'nuclear family'. Both use notions of culture and tradition to reaffirm women's status as subordinate to men, curtailing female economic and political participation.

Ways of working on culture

Even where gender ideologies succeed in restricting women's freedom of expression, participation, and mobility, women typically have many and varied strategies to combat these limitations. Maitrayee Mukhopadhyay asserts in her article that the cultural biases of Northern development agencies incline them to ignore 'the everyday forms of resistance put up by subordinated groups, because these forms of resistance don't fit our experiences'.

A common charge levelled at gender and development practitioners is that gender equity is a 'Western' concern, and is neither needed nor desired by Southern women. This view can itself be seen to be an example of cultural bias. Sara Longwe asserts: 'obviously, if women are very oppressed and suppressed, they are also very silent.' Hearing the discontent of subordinated groups depends on the willingness to seek them out, and listen.

The testimony of Rehana Khatun Adeer, who works with DISHA (a social organisation in Uttar Pradesh, India, which has received long-term funding from Oxfam), gives a glimpse of the degree of social change, on both individual and community levels, which may occur through women's participation in development projects. Rehana Khatun Adeer challenged her seclusion, and the demands of her husband's family that she wear an all-enveloping *bourkha*, in order to take part in research for DISHA. Her involvement in the research has changed not only her own life, but also her extended family's view of women's status, abilities, and strength.

While such participation enables women to challenge their marginalisation within their communities, it also provides inspiration for other women. Collettah Chitsike, who works for Oxfam in Zimbabwe, points out that such positive female role-models can convince women and men that women's empowerment is a legitimate goal.

Popular culture and gender equity

Addressing the cultural basis of women's subordination requires recognition of the means by which we are socialised to accept, and perpetuate, a reductive image of women's achievements and capacities. Gramsci, the Italian philosopher and politician, identifies popular culture as a critical means of reinforcing the ruling ideas which define social relations (Simon 1991). While acknowledging the power of the arts and media to perpetuate existing discrimination, we need to grasp the opportunities that the arts and media offer us, to challenge the status quo.

Alzira Rufino is a feminist activist and founder of the first black women's cultural centre in Brazil. In an interview with her, Katrina Payne explored her views on the need to strengthen the aspects of culture and tradition which are beneficial for all members of society, not only those who currently have power. Valuing our particular cultural heritage should lead to a respect for the heritage of other people, rather than to a feeling of our own superiority. In this way, respect for culture as the essential history of a society is grounded on a commitment to justice and fairness to all members of our own society, and of others.

In her article, Adrianna Santa Cruz discusses how one Latin American initiative, Fempress, has been a focus for women activists by providing publications and radio run by women, for women. In addition to raising awareness of women's struggle for equality, Fempress has proved to be an effective means for women to set up networks, thereby strengthening alliances in the women's movement.

Defining multiculturalism

Just as women's views have been marginalised by men, the views of the South have been marginalised by the North, and the voices of people with a formal education are heard above those of people who have experience, but lack qualifications. In their article, Abena Busia and Seble Dawit argue that this 'selective listening' has continued within the women's movement. They assert that the values and aspirations of the South, and particularly of Southern women, have been largely ignored by Northern feminists, academics, and practitioners.

The ideal of multiculturalism requires international development agencies to listen to Southern voices, and particularly to those which have historically been ignored, on the assumption that the rulers of a society, or the male household head, speaks for all. In her article, Chitsike discusses how it feels to be a Southern woman working for a Northern funding agency, and what the term 'multicultur-alism' means to her.

Social development is a process which is incompatible with the short-term project approach of Northern-based development planning. As Colletah Chitsike points out, changing social relations so that subor-dinated members of a community have their voices heard necessitates a commit-ment of resources on a long-term basis. Development initiatives should not only take note of the need for long-term commitment to changing culture, but to the need to employ local people, like Rehana Khatun Adeer of DISHA, wherever possible.

However, the ideal of multiculturalism can be perverted if the notion of culture is used as a justification for practices which violate the rights of oppressed groups. In her article, Sara Longwe provides answers to the charges of 'interference' in the culture of sovereign states, which may be brought against international development agencies which seek to promote gender equity in their development work. Unquestioning respect for the integrity of a culture carries a danger of 'cultural relativism': the idea that there are no universal concepts of human rights. As Busia and Dawit observe, charges of cultural imperialism can be refuted only if the aspirations of Southern women set the agenda for development work with a gender perspective.

Caroline Sweetman

References

Amoah E (1987) 'Women, witches and social change in Ghana' in *Speaking of Faith: Cross-cultural Perspectives on Women and Social Change* (ed Eck D and Jain D) Kali For Women.

Armstrong K (1986) *The Gospel According to Woman*, Elm Tree Books/Hamish Hamilton Ltd.

Hall S (1992) 'Introduction' in *Formations of Modernity*, (ed Hall S and Gieben B) Polity Press/Open University.

Levinson (1989) *Family Violence in Cross-Cultural Perspective*, Sage Publications.

Moraga C (1988) 'From a long line of vendidas: chicanas and feminism', in *Feminist Studies/Cultural Studies*, (ed. de Laurentis T)

O'Connell H (1994) *Women and the family*, Zed Books.

Simon R (1991) *Gramsci's Political Thought: An Introduction*, Lawrence and Wishart.

UNESCO (undated) *The Cultural Dimensions of Development: Towards a Practical Approach*, UNESCO Publishing.

MIKE EDWARD/OXFAM

Women's group in Zimbabwe. A sense of shared culture is a powerful cohesive force, giving a sense of identity and group solidarity.

Thinking about 'culture': some programme pointers

Seble Dawit and Abena Busia

This article is a collaboration, from a lawyer and a poet, on those aspects of being 'Southern' or 'Third World' women which seem most important when we think about how to transform culture, from a gender perspective.

In order to consider culture in the programme work of development agencies, it is necessary for development workers to examine their own cultural heritage, and recognise that the way we look at the world is affected by our own experience of race, class/caste, sexuality, and gender. We need to learn to take this subjectivity into account in our daily lives and activities. Transformation, whether individual or institutional, must always begin with us looking at ourselves and our reactions to what goes on around us.

Culturally-based attitudes to race and ethnicity are among the most difficult to challenge. Precisely because we all view our own cultural assumptions as the norm, it is difficult to bring to the fore the impact of these assumptions. Cultural subjectivity flavours both the North/South dialogue attempted by Oxfam in its Women's Linking Project (Oxfam, 1994), and the South/South dialogues that are essential for an understanding of gender and development. Gender discrimination is global, but unless racial and ethnic biases in the context of North/South dialogue are confronted, the various manifestations of

gender discrimination within different communities can be neither recognised, nor dealt with.

This is not an argument for 'cultural relativism', which asserts that each society has its own values which must be judged in their specific context. We must question the normative idea of the white liberal feminist, and the assumption held by such feminists that gender oppression is the primary (and only) ground of struggle. While acknowledging that gender oppression is universal, it is imperative to avoid what Gayatri Spivak terms the spectacle of 'White women saving Brown women from Brown men' (Spivak, 1988). Acknowledging the importance of taking race and ethnicity into account allows us to challenge firmly what Mohanty calls 'the authorising signature of Western humanist discourse' (Mohanty 1991).

There are certainly many culturally legitimised practices, harmful to women, which some women have challenged, within their own communities, and will continue to fight. But there will be tensions if outsiders attempt to dictate to people about their cultural practices. What must be respected is that it is the Southern women themselves who, tired of being unveiled, rescued from fires, or inspected between the legs, have done a great deal of self-empowering work to combat those situations, and whose understanding of their cultural roots result in powerful analyses based on their first-hand experience.

Examining cultural constructs

Much of the tension aroused by Northern attempts to address aspects of Southern cultural practice is rooted in the way in which Western academics have shaped their view of the South as alien and 'other'. The very language we use shapes the way in which we see the world:

An old Englishman I met in Africa was reminiscing about his exploration in earlier days, and the shock of one culture meeting another for the first time. 'Can you imagine', he said, 'people so primitive that they love to eat the embryo of certain birds and slices from the belly of certain animals? And grind up grass seed, make it into a paste, burn it over a fire, then smear it with a greasy mess they extract from the mammary fluid of animals?' While I shuddered at such barbarism, he went on: 'What I've been describing, of course, is a breakfast of bacon and eggs, and buttered toast.' (Gaskill 1964)

Western organisations must make the effort to examine cultural, including linguistic, practices which shape their own world view, as rigorously as they do those in Southern societies. A culture can only be understood in its political, social, and economic context.

We should examine aspects of unfamiliar cultures bearing in mind that they serve a purpose, even if the nature of this purpose remains unclear to us. Cultural dictates are social structures based on economic and political needs. Though the rise of a particular cultural practice can rarely be traced back to a precise economic or political cause, the way in which such practices are promoted and protected within the community shows their purpose. As the Ghanaian philosopher W E Abraham notes, '... culture is the common life of the people... [Whatever it] may not do, at least it puts a bridle on individualism...[and serves an] integrative function...' (Abraham, 1962)

Within the context of a given culture there are norms that guide the behaviour of individuals and of the community as a whole. These norms may be simplified into rights and responsibilities, firstly, of individuals to each other, and, secondly, between individuals and the community. Cultures are co-operative systems, whose *raison d'être* is the survival and perpetuation of the community. One of the issues which distinguish cultures in North and South is that, in general, Northern societies tend to encourage behaviour based on a sense of personal individualism whereas, for the most part, Southern cultures are still organised on communal lines. While the North may question the limitations of such a collective identity, it should realise that its own standpoint is not objective, but is, like that of the South, a product of culture. When speaking of cultural dictates and practices in relation to women, we very often find ourselves questioning the extent of a community's efforts to govern the behaviour of individuals, and its right to do so.

Gender issues and culture

Gender identity is a social construction, whose rationale is related to the biological difference between the sexes. The way in which gender identity is formed reflects the particular needs and world view of each society. Culture and gender are thus intertwined, interdependent, and mutually defining to a certain extent.

It is an acknowledged factor that in nearly all civilisations women have been viewed as 'guardians of the culture'. This remains true even when, if viewed from the outside, certain aspects of the culture can be said to be harmful to women. Underlying such anomaly is the general view of cultural practices as beneficial to society, and the privilege accorded to those who conform to the culture by practising and maintaining it.

While there is a great deal of work being done to address the most oppressive and harmful aspects of culture as it affects women, there is a danger that the very important and difficult work of defining local needs and setting agendas based on them will be subsumed by indignation which is not based on an analysis of the cultural context. Compare the extremely informative work and writings of local and regional activists on female genital mutilation in parts of Africa, and dowry death and sati in the Indian Sub-continent.[1]

We must be aware of the risks of a cross-cultural dialogue which, while trying to highlight similarities, and ground for women's solidarity and concerted action, actually ignores critical cross-cultural differences in the economic and political bases of women's oppression. If we group together all aspects of culture which present problems for women under the title 'harmful cultural practices', the danger is that this may result in an assumption that the impetus for each oppressive practice is the same; it might seem, therefore, that the solutions should be equally transferable.

Instead, when we consider the relationship of gender issues and culture, we must start by viewing each situation as unique, and only then consider the similarities between it and other situations; not the other way round. We must ground our work on culture and gender in an awareness of the need to look at the precise context of harmful practices. It may seem an academic point, but part of the process of learning how to think about culture is to change radically the ways in which we are trained to think.

Let us consider two cultural practices which have a negative impact upon women. On the face of it, the 'reason' for the existence of female infanticide in China and female foeticide in India is identical: the over-riding preference for male children (Hom, 1992, on China, and Cheetu, 1991, on India). Below the surface, however, different historical, political, economic, and social factors come into play, laying the basis for these practices. There is at least one notable difference between foeticide in India and infanticide in China, namely, the attitude of the State. Though India permits abortion, the Indian government has outlawed the use of amniocentesis as a basis for female foeticide. China, on the other hand, has a stringent one-child population policy.

We need to ask ourselves the following questions: at what historical moment might such practices have come into being? What are the social and economic demands that perpetuate them? Is class a factor in the prevalence of oppressive practices? What combination of social, economic, and political changes might diminish the incidence of these practices? How do local people understand and explain them?

The responses to these questions, among others, reveal the differences between practices which are similar, but not identical. It is the differences, and not the similarities, which will determine the specific steps to be taken towards defining a programme to address the problem, which has a good chance of success.

Recommendations for action

Women from different parts of the world may be approaching the question of culture from different angles, but there seems to be a general agreement that tackling gender oppression based in culture necessitates enabling women to empower themselves and raise their status in their societies; it cannot be achieved only by raising women's consciousness of their oppression.

The emphasis in development initiatives should be on long-term investment, as opposed to short-term results, since meeting the development goal of furnishing basic needs means that cultural norms and gender biases must be identified and addressed, to ensure that women as well as men have the resources they need: adequate nutrition, employment, credit, housing, and health care. Altering culture is by definition a long-term process.

Cultural considerations cut across all the major themes currently being addressed by development agencies: it is very difficult to generalise about the different sorts of work being done to challenge those aspects of culture which have a damaging effect on women. In Asia, there is an emphasis on general literacy, and legal literacy in particular, as a means of raising women's consciousness as well as enabling them to bring about change through knowledge of their rights. In Latin America, there is a strong focus on women's reproductive health care, and freedom from gender-based violence.[2] In many parts of Africa, much work is being done around HIV/AIDS in relation to women, including the effects of the disease on members of the family, the care of orphans, cultural practices that put women at higher risk, and legal remedies for destitute families.[3]

There needs to be more support for long-term research and programmes on attitude-change about gender issues and the status of women among women, men, girls, and boys. There is a need for more research on the knowledge of, attitudes to, and practice of, harmful manifestations of culture.

Illiteracy is intricately tied to the overall problem of the low status of women in most parts of the world. If any lasting positive change is to be brought about in the status of women, the illiteracy rates for women and girls must be brought down. The United Nations estimates that, while illiteracy rates have dropped, increases in population have caused the actual numbers of illiterate women and girls to increase (United Nations, 1991). The work of literacy organisations is, therefore, critical to diminishing the negative impact of traditional gender roles. But literacy is not the work of these organisations alone. Any donor considering a proposal and any grantee preparing one should ask themselves: where is the education in this?

This is particularly urgent for Southern women's NGOs, who do not have the luxury of focusing all of their efforts on one

PETER COLERIDGE/OXFAM

Young reader, Andhra Pradesh. Literacy is of great importance in enabling women to bring about change, through knowledge of their legal rights.

issue. It is imperative, therefore, that health clinics not only provide services but also provide some sexual and general health education. Projects for economic activities and empowerment may provide information on how the larger economy functions. Such project-specific literacy does not demand extra time of women, is more immediately useful to them, and involves them in the work of the service they are patronising.

It is in the very nature of Oxfam as a donor institution, or charity, that the flow of material resources is from Oxfam in the North to us in the South. There are in-built cultural assumptions about this North-South flow, which need to be recognised in creating a true sense of partnership. A key to facilitating, and building upon, interaction between a donor agency such as Oxfam and local NGOs working on gender issues is local agenda setting. Often, donor-driven initiatives are frustrating for both donor and receivers. While the former wants results, but often lacks knowledge as to what is truly feasible, the latter need support to do the kind of work they feel is appropriate and useful. In trying to come to an understanding, either one or both often settles for work that they do not find useful.

When women's groups are allowed to guide the development of their own programmes, an investment is made in local capacity-building. Organisations working on the same issue, such as reproductive rights, should be encouraged to link up, as should organisations working on related issues. In this way, information can be shared, and can have an impact upon those who are the target beneficiaries of programmes, as well as educating providers about relevant work on gender issues that they may have neither the time nor the inclination to examine themselves.

Women's organisations must also contribute their own efforts to this linking initiative. Larger NGOs might, for example, run workshops on writing proposals and reports, and can educate and inform each other on a reciprocal basis. For example, legal services and legal information may be offered to a health-care organisation in exchange for allowing the health workers the opportunity to give health education to women in the legal-aid waiting room. There are local groups already connecting in innovative ways, but these collaborations need to be encouraged by funding agencies, and formalised as programmes where possible (Rao, 1991).

Relationships between women's NGOs and traditional NGOs should also be encouraged, to ensure that work on women's issues is not marginalised. Ideally, a gender component would be integrated into the work of every NGO because, ultimately, women need to be recognised as an integral part of every major programme area and the social system as a whole.

The following are general recommendations for governments:

- integration of a gender component into the work of every Ministry and not merely the creation of a Women's Ministry;
- more emphasis on literacy for girls and women, including implementation of laws on the education of school-age girls;
- public support for local women's initiatives, such as childcare centres, women's shelters, small business co-operatives, community health services, and legal aid services;
- training in gender-sensitivity for judges, police, teachers, clerics, and students of law and medicine;
- more and urgent attention to the particular situation, status, and needs of adolescent and young women;
- more women in visible official posts in public service.

In conclusion, we must keep in mind that, while the above are general guidelines for programme activities, the definitions that are ultimately relied on during the development of individual programmes must come from communities themselves (Alexander, 1990). Whether the interest is to strengthen or question culture and tradition, the approach needs to be based on indigenous knowledge, and not on external perceptions of that knowledge.

Notes

1   On the former, see Mohammed A'Haleem, A (1992) 'Claiming our bodies and our rights: exploring female circumcision as an act of violence in Africa', in Schuler, M (ed) *Freedom From Violence: Women's Strategies from Around the World*; Koso-Thomas, O (1987) *The Circumcision of Women: A Strategy for Eradication*, Zed Books, London; Walker, A (1993) *Warrior Marks: Genital Mutilation and the Sexual Blinding of Women*, Harcourt Brace, New York; Hosken, F P (1979) *The Hosken Report on Genital and Sexual Mutilation of Females*, WIN News. On the latter, see Cheetu, S (1991) 'Growing menace of female foeticide in India', *Indian Socio-Legal Journal*, 17: 1 and 2, pp. 76-86; Newman, E (1992) 'For richer for poorer, till death do us part: India's response to dowry deaths', *International Law Student Assoc. Journal of International Law*, 15, pp. 109-143.

2   See, among others, the work of organisations such as Flora Tristan in Peru, SOS Corpo in Brazil, CEFEMINA in Costa Rica, ISIS in Chile.

3   See generally, Lamptey, P and Piot, P (1990) *The Handbook of AIDS Prevention in Africa*, Family Health International, Durham, NC; Obbo, C (1993) 'Reflections on the AIDS orphans problem in Uganda' in Berer, M and Ray, S (eds) *Women and HIV/AIDS: An International Resource Book*, Pandora Press, London. See also the legal aid work of the Uganda Women Lawyer's Association.

Bibliography

Abraham, W E (1962) *The Mind of Africa*, University of Chicago Press, p. 21.

Alexander, J (1990) 'Mobilising against the State and international "aid" agencies: "Third World" women define reproductive freedom' in Fried M G (ed) *From Abortion to Reproductive Freedom: Transforming a Movement*, South End Press, Boston.

Cheetu, S (1991) 'Growing menace of female foeticide in India', in *Indian Socio-Legal Journal*, 17: 1 and 2, p. 76

Crick, M (1976) 'The translation of cultures', Chapter 8 in *Explorations in Language and Meaning: Towards a Semantic Anthropology*, Malaby Press, London, p. 166.

Gaskill, G (March 1964), from *Reader's Digest*.

Hom, S K (1992) 'Female infanticide in China: the human rights specter and thoughts towards (an)other vision', in *Columbia Human Rights Law Review*, 23: 2, Summer; p. 249.

Oxfam (1994) 'Women Linking For Change: Oxfam's women's linking project', *Focus on Gender*, 2: 3, Oxfam, Oxford.

Rao, A (1991) 'Incorporating gender issues into development training', Rao, A (ed) *Women's Studies International: Nairobi and Beyond*, The Feminist Press, New York, p. 129.

Spivak, G C (1988) 'Can the subaltern speak?' in Nelson, C and Grossberg, L (eds) *Marxism and the Interpretation of Culture*, Urbana: University of Illinois Press, pp. 271-313.

Mohanty, T, Chandra, Russo, A and Torres, L (eds) (1991) *Third World Women and the Politics of Feminism*, Indiana University Press, Bloomington.

United Nations (1991) *The World's Women*, p. 45.

Gender relations, development practice and 'culture'

Maitrayee Mukhopadhyay

This article analyses the dilemmas faced by development practitioners when dealing with the issue of gender relations, and the way in which these are rooted in different cultures. 'Insiders' can be accused of treachery to their own culture, and 'outsiders' of a lack of cultural sensitivity.

Dilemmas concerning gender and culture have implications for both development theory and practice, because all development practitioners are in some way intervening in processes of social transformation, and are involved in the critical business of allocating resources. Thus, what development practitioners believe to be the nature of gender relations in a specific cultural context, and how they view 'culture' in general, has practical consequences; their understanding of gender and culture can further entrench gender inequality, or demonstrate the possibility that such inequalities are open to challenge.

What are some of the dilemmas regarding gender and culture, and how do these determine the eventual allocation of resources in development work? The starting point is to look at the questions that practitioners tend to be asked, and the allegations against them that are made when development initiatives are perceived to be interfering in the critical area of gender relations.

Before doing this, in the best traditions of feminist practice and politics, I will begin from my personal perspective, by stating my own position in the debate. I am an Indian feminist, and have been a development practitioner for almost 15 years. As a development activist, the understanding of development which has informed my work is that it is about distributive justice. Thus, hierarchies of caste, class, race, and gender have constantly to be challenged in order to ensure that the goal of equity remains in the foreground. As a feminist, I see my role as opening up the most intimate area of life — social relations, including kinship, family, and conjugal relations — in order to challenge gender oppression.

Issues of identity

In my work in India, I was operating within my own society and culture, and so was speaking as an 'insider'. Despite this, it was in my work for gender equity that I most often experienced allegations from different quarters that this work was against our culture, violated our traditions, and, the worst criticism of all in the Indian context, that it was 'Westernised'.

It is a common experience of development practitioners working on gender issues to be labelled in this manner, although the way questions are posed and allegations made may differ from country to country and region to region. The common basis of the allegations is that gender relations are viewed as among the most intimate aspects of our cultural traditions, and challenging these seems to challenge the very basis of who we are.

Why is this, and how does it constrain us? Before we can proceed to look at the hows and whys, I will share some of my own experiences, to highlight the issues. In 1984, I published a book concerned with women and development in India. I was invited by Oxfam, my publishers, to undertake a publicity tour in the United Kingdom. Among the many presentations I made, the most memorable for me was the one at the Pakistan Centre in Liverpool. Most of the predominantly male audience were of South Asian origin, from India, Pakistan, and Bangladesh.

The discussion that followed my talk was lively, to say the least, and abusive at its worst. In fact, I became afraid of being lynched. My book criticised the Indian model of development, for having worked against women's interests, and Indian society, for its treatment of women. I was initially taken aback by the reaction, until it began to dawn on me what was happening. The Indians, Pakistanis, and Bangladeshis had united (leaving aside, for the time being, their bitter nationalist enmities on the sub-continent) in a vigorous defence of culture and tradition; a tradition which respected its women, a tradition which was protective of its women, a tradition in which women were the centre of families which, in turn, were collectivities of mutual co-operation, love, and sacrifice. In fact, the polarised, simplified picture of gender relations that was being drawn amounted to a fiction of a monolithic, timeless culture; an immutable, 'South Asian' culture.

Bangladesh: the ideal vision of women at the centre of a tightly-knit, co-operative family group is a strong element of South Asian culture

CLARE HANSON-KHAN/OXFAM

I had offended my audience firstly, by 'turning traitor' to my own culture, and raising doubts about women's position in Indian society. Secondly, I had done so in a 'Western country' which they had decided to perceive, in the interests of preserving their own separate cultural identity, as a culture which was full of 'loose' women, and broken families.

As an interesting sequel to this experience, a Pakistani woman followed me out of the hall, and thanked me for my presentation. She was working with Asian women facing domestic violence; she had become involved in this work when her daughter had committed suicide, unable to endure any longer the harassment and torture she had suffered in her marital home.

Assumptions about culture

The reactions which I experienced on that occasion are not limited to Asian communities living abroad. Throughout the 1980s, as the women's movement in India strove to put equitable gender relations on the agenda of politicians and development agencies, feminist activists were faced with the same questions and accusations. It was alleged that we were destroying the family, the very edifice on which our culture was built, a culture which had survived for centuries.

I am often asked, usually by expatriate development workers, whether by intervening on women's behalf we are upsetting the gender roles and relations characteristic of the culture. In other words, are we fearful of imposing our own culture on the culture in which we are working, by initiating projects which impact on gender relations? Are we not leaving women more vulnerable than before, by asking them to step out of their culturally ascribed roles and relations?

The assumptions behind these questions need a close examination. Firstly, it is assumed that the culture of communities we work in as development practitioners are a seamless whole, without any cracks; secondly, that unequal gender relations characterise these cultures, and that there are no challenges to inequality from within the cultures. In fact, it is assumed that to be a woman in such cultures is to be passive, subservient, and servile. The passive and subservient woman, who is also a victim, thus becomes the stereotype of these cultures.

The fear that we may be imposing our own cultural values by insisting on promoting gender equity in our development work is a real one. However, it is real not because we have concerns about cultural imperialism, but because we allow our own culture-based assumptions about women to colour the way we receive alternative visions of gender equality. We assume that women in developing countries are passive and docile, and that our own view of gender roles, norms, and practices is true for everyone. We also fail to recognise the everyday forms of resistance put up by subordinated groups, because these forms of resistance may not correspond to our experience.

Culture and religion

Another set of assumptions about culture and gender relations are rooted in religious concerns. Religion, we are told, is the basis for many of the cultural values which prescribe what women are and how they should behave, how they should relate to each other, and what is permissible or impermissible for women to do. It is often alleged that, by advocating gender equality through development programmes, we are 'interfering in religion'. The inference of this is that development practitioners should be respectful of the norms and prescriptions of what purports to be a 'religion'.

What are the assumptions behind these claims? First, there is the assumption that religion is the only basis of the culture of a people; indeed, the term 'religion' is often used interchangeably with culture. Second, that followers of a religion, no matter where they happen to live in the world, practise it in the same way and are governed by exactly the same rules of social interaction irrespective of the social, political, and economic differences in their situations.

Religion is thus reconfirmed as unchanging and unchangeable, and prescriptive about gender roles. People are assumed to be slavishly subservient to their religion; this unquestioning loyalty to religion is viewed as more common in 'traditional' cultures than 'modern' ones. For example, this slavish subservience to religion is rarely, if ever, used to describe Western culture.

DAVE THOMSON/OXFAM

Bathing festival, Varanasi. Religion and culture are closely linked, and those advocating gender equality may be accused of attacking religion

Exploding the myths

If we survey all these dilemmas about working on gender and culture, we get a fair picture of the notions of culture held by the majority of development practitioners. First, gender relations are somehow equated with the most intimate aspects of our cultures. Second, culture and tradition are seen as immutable and unchanging. Third, the notion of the need for development practitioners to work in a 'culturally sensitive' way implies that the culture of a community is one where there is no resistance from subordinated groups. Fourth, that religion *is* culture.

It is obvious how these notions about culture serve as constraints on working for equitable gender relations. Gender relations become a 'no-go area', and allocating resources in a way that redresses the imbalance of power between men and women is made politically difficult.

If, as development practitioners, we share a general understanding that development is about redistributive justice and equity, then we must look for ways to overcome the constraints imposed upon us by these false notions of culture and gender relations. The best way to do this is by examining whether the assumptions about culture have empirical validity.

In order to test the validity of these common assumptions about culture and gender relations, I would like to analyse the experience I had in 1984 and which I have described above. Readers may find that my experience reminds them of similar experiences in their own work on culture and gender. The experience brought home to me the importance of cultural identity, and the vastly complicated way in which culture works.

How did the men who attacked my views understand the cultural identity of South Asia? Their notions of culture are built on the idea of South Asian families being all alike. Central to the view of the perfect family is the ideal of womanhood, and the gender relations which stem from this. The family is depicted as a unit of mutual interest, love, and co-operation, within which women are respected.

However, this family unity depends on the subsuming of women's interests. The distinct social identity of the perfect South Asian family is also defined by the idea of the Western family as 'other'. This idea of family becomes the emblem of an entire culture: it is seen as immutable, timeless, and almost primordial. The meaning of what it is to be Indian is represented by the idea of the tightly-woven family unit.

The meaning of what it is to be South Asian, represented by the notion of the family as a unit of mutual interest, is challenged by the real life experience of women who are abused, and who are not willing to put up with this abuse. It is torn

apart by the experiences related to me by the woman who congratulated me on my presentation. Presenting the family in this way obscures the hierarchies that exist within it: hierarchies of gender, and of age. Because the idea of family is perceived as an unchanging, universal ideal, it also obscures the fact that the meanings of male and female identities, and of 'family', are constantly being contested, and are changed in the process.

Working with culture

How do these observations provide answers to the dilemmas that development practitioners face in relation to culture and gender? Perhaps it would help to appreciate that, since cultural meanings have constantly to be constructed and reconstructed in order to lend significance to social practices, no culture stands still. Cultures are not fixed or immutable.

ALISON BARRETT/OXFAM

Women stage a protest march in Bangladesh. The posters read 'an end to violence against women'.

Contests to 'fix' the meanings of social entities take place all the time, leading to changes in social practices. The point is to recognise what these contests are about, and how they operate to change social meanings.

The implication of the above for gender and development practitioners is that we have to take sides in those contests which help to dismantle hierarchies of gender and class. By failing to recognise that contests take place, and listening only to the voice of the powerful in society, we are unwittingly taking the side of the fundamentalists, who render religion uniform throughout the world by

Cultures are not fixed or immutable. Contests to 'fix' the meanings of social entities take place all the time, leading to changes in social practices.

enforcing traditions of hierarchical gender roles and relations, and presenting these as unchanging and authoritative. We are also siding with nationalists, who use the same 'traditions' to construct ethnic boundaries, and, finally, with states who use the excuse of culture not to address the secular violence faced by women.

Cultural theorists have been at pains to point out that cultures undergo processes of evolution. These seem less tangible and more abstract than political and economic processes, because they deal with meanings, values, identities, symbols, ideas, knowledge, language, ideology. However, they make up the world we live in, and we recreate them in our turn.

In fact, economic and political processes also depend on the significance and interpretation attached to them by different cultures. For example, the market economy requires new ideas about economic life, just as it requires new organisational forms. All social practices have significance according to the prevailing culture. Since this significance cannot be fixed for all time, but undergoes constant change, those working for social development must recognise that there are no hard and fast distinctions between the material world, and the world of ideas, values, and beliefs. We must work at both levels, if we are to achieve the desired changes that development is supposed to bring about.

I end with a plea that development practitioners use culture as a way to open up intractable areas of gender relations, and do not regard culture as a dead-end, which prevents us from working towards more equitable gender relations.

Finally, a word about working with 'cultural sensitivity', generally understood to mean respect for the given norms of a culture. Concern for cultural sensitivity is sparked off by the dilemmas about culture which this article has tried to explore. A new definition of cultural sensitivity, and its application in situations where gender relations are at stake, would be to acknowledge that there are contests around the significance attached by a society to different aspects of social constructs, and that often these contests represent challenges to hierarchical social relations.

Maitrayee Mukhopadhyay is Gender Adviser for Oxfam, focusing on South Asia and the Middle East.

NGOs, gender, culture and multiculturalism

a Zimbabwean view

Colleta Chitsike

Women across the globe experience gender oppression in many, and different, ways. Colleta Chitsike refuses to see the fight against gender injustices as a 'Northern' concept. As a woman from the 'South', she sees gender injustice as it affects her personally, as well as the ways in which it affects other women.

Several times in my professional life, when I have been working with male colleagues, they have expected me, as a woman, to serve them. For example, after a long day working with partners in the rural areas, when the meal is served in the village, my male colleagues have often expected me to fetch water to wash their hands, and to divide the food for them. Their work is only to put the food into their mouths. It never occurs to them that we have all been doing the same work, and that we are all tired. Sometimes male colleagues even believe your real purpose is to service them sexually, and when one refuses their sexual advances, they say one is 'Westernised'.

On a number of occasions I have heard male colleagues saying they would never marry an educated woman: they claim educated black women have lost their knowledge of 'cultural practices', and they do not know the practices of the other culture they have taken on — therefore they are viewed as confused. Women who challenge gender injustice as it exists in our culture are called prostitutes and accused of failing in their duties to housekeeping

and in their marriages. Even churches will preach that women who want to enter male domains are deviating from what is normal and acceptable — they quote Genesis, Chapter 2. Women always have to try twice as hard as men to be accepted if they step out of the narrow role assigned to them by culture.

When someone says the word 'gender', it first makes me think of women being made aware of their problems in a male-dominated society, realising that what they can do and cannot do is determined not by their abilities, but by their gender i.e. the expectations people have from a woman or man because they are physically female or male. Secondly, 'gender' makes me think of the negative self-image which I carried for a long time deep inside me, as I grew up. At primary school level, I was made to feel worthless, weaker and smaller than the boys. This was new to me as I had no brothers at home, and therefore had no feeling of inferiority to any sibling.

Subsequently, I spent time in the nursing profession, where a system of unequal power relations between women and men was crosscut by other injustices caused by race, class, tribe, and culture. Because of these other divisions, women subordinated and oppressed other women in many ways. Petty jealousies and regimental systems of ranks created extreme competition, and terrible power struggles, in institutions. White men and women oppressed black people, and the black middle and upper classes oppressed poor black people, including the sick.

It was at this period that I learnt that oppression is maintained by our social systems, and it is almost impossible for one person to challenge it single-handedly. I went on to university to study Adult Education, which emphasises the principle of working within democratic frameworks in educational programmes based on the concerns of the learners. This brought many issues to light for me.

First, it is an accepted fact that women are globally subordinate, particularly in socio-economic and symbolic power, to men. Women's subordination is rooted in customs and beliefs that are produced or shared by particular societies. Because of the historical status accorded to a woman, many societies expect women to be submissive, obedient to father, brother or husband and his male relatives, sometimes even to her own son. Women are generally regarded as inferior to men both physically and intellectually, and are therefore treated with contempt.

Some women choose to ignore gender injustice. For example, many Zimbabwean women will state that it is 'cultural' for women to be subordinate to men. What is 'cultural' about a woman earning all the food through her sweat in the fields, and preparing that food for her husband and children to sustain them when the man is drinking the day away? Is it 'cultural' to be beaten to pulp and protect the man who has done it? The questions can go on and on — there is a vast world literature on

CHRIS JOHNSON/OXFAM

Preparing the ground for a food crop, Zambia. 'Cultural tradition' is often used to justify women's heavy workloads.

what women suffer in the name of culture.

Attitudes towards women as being inferior and lesser human beings at all levels, are reinforced directly or indirectly in many complex ways. People who oppress others tend to share a belief in their own 'natural' superiority: it is actually 'culture' which justifies this belief. Many men think because they are male they have the right to own women and oppress them in all kinds of ways — from owning them as part of their estate, to battering and raping women to show their dominance, and to humiliate women.

According to Zimbabwean tradition, when a man dies, his wife is inherited by a male relative of the late husband — either one of his brothers or one of his nephews. If a woman's son is her husband's heir, she becomes subservient to her own son. Stories of sons throwing their mothers into the streets after a father dies are not uncommon. Deeply embedded cultural beliefs cause many women to think that in order to be free from the man's spirit, cleansing practices must be carried out. One such practice takes place one year after death, where the families gather together and sing and drink all night, before taking some beer to the grave. In some ethnic groups, this practice also includes the widow having sex with a relative of her dead husband on the same night.

Stimulating social change

The cultural differences which exist in the way gender oppression manifests itself from society to society are often not understood by Northern activists, who may think that a practice like this is simply barbaric and should be done away with forthwith. But changing cultural practices takes a long time. To erode discrimination

JACQUIE MONTY/OXFAM

Women's group meeting, Zambia. 'Many women will speak and behave positively when in a group.'
Women's groups can provide powerful support for challenging oppressive cultural practices

against women, which is a very complex, deeply rooted injustice, we need a multifaceted, explosive force that can shake individuals to change their attitudes and to inspire women as individuals, to make them want to tackle this injustice. Women of the peasantry, as well as urban working-class women, need to understand and devise ways of living outside the bounds imposed by the patriarchal culture.

There is need for more role models of strong women ... who will inspire other women

Generally, male-dominated society will emphasise women's subordination in its laws and notions of 'tradition', whereas in reality customs may exist that give a certain degree of power to women. Often these positive roles that women play traditionally are not reflected in popular views of 'culture'. For example, historically Zimbabwean women have held decision-making positions as spirit mediums, and in chieftainships, but this tends to be ignored. It is important to acknowledge that women can and do challenge culture, and that some women have been able to assert their own views and maintain a certain amount of independence from patriarchal values and practices. As the challenge to gender injustice becomes stronger, those that perpetuate gender injustice are in turn becoming stronger and more ruthless in promoting practices that render women powerless.

Women need to take in what is positive from the community and culture, and reject what is negative and harming their lives; it is important to proceed slowly and allow women themselves to realise this for themselves. As an activist, I listen to each group of women and proceed at a pace which will assist them to realise their oppression. In this way, they take me

seriously, as an agent of change who genuinely wishes good for them, and not to destroy them.

To change aspects of culture which are harmful to women requires a process which is sensitive, persuasive, non-threatening, and carefully planned to take into account the problems faced by the women, and how they perceive those problems. Popular education is one way of creating awareness among women of their oppression. Developed because of dissatisfaction with other models of education, popular education arose as a result of challenging the way people were taught in schools — a way that silenced learners and made them conform. Adult education arose from similar thinking, that adults need a different methodology and different climate in order for them to change.

Popular education is about collective learning and takes a political stand on the role of marginalised people; women, as the group suffering the effects of gender oppression, can gain strength from learning collectively and sharing their experiences of problems. Methods of education that encourage individual discovery within the group promote women's confidence, self-respect, and determination to do something about injustice and to improve women's status.

Role models

Many women will speak and behave positively when in a group, whereas, when they are confronted individually, they display a totally different picture due to pressure to conform to women's subservient gender role, in the family and in personal relationships. As a result there are few positive role models of women who challenge gender roles.

Popular education takes into account role modelling through training for transformation where both activist and learner are transformed. There is need for more role models of strong women: it is they who will inspire other women, and help them to change their negative self-image. However, women who are positive role models must be aware that they will risk suffering trauma in the process since they are deviating from normal female behaviour. If more women took up this challenge, then more children would learn from their mothers' example, and more sons will grow up realising that the potential they and their sisters have is equal.

My own experience of being a role model is that some of the learning which occurs is caused by spontaneous actions, for example, when a community sees a woman doing things that are not tradition-ally done by women in those communities. I worked with another woman on the Rural Malawi Oxfam Mulanje Community Training Programme: it was amazing how many small successes we achieved through being seen as two women working success-fully for an international organisation.

Comments were along the lines of: 'Where did Oxfam get two highly competent women who can cope without a man to guide them? How come you can drive on these dangerous roads at night?' Village communities often came up with questions such as 'These women, how can they possibly cope?' In one village, a chief challenged a male colleague to take over the driving, saying that it was not good to show the village women that women are capable of driving, because they would get 'wrong ideas about what they can do and what they should aim for'.

Others realised the positive aspects of women's empowerment: a father of nine daughters asked me to drive up to his doorstep, so that I would show his daughters and his wife that women are capable, and can do many jobs that men do. 'Look at this woman, is she not managing her own life? Why do you want to keep having children, so that you try to get a son? God has given us nine girls, let us encourage them not to have babies but send them to school — they'll look after us better if they are educated and education will take them out of poverty.' This family became friends of mine, and through this kind of interaction more people are affected, because they talk about it to their own relations. Not everyone will be won instantly by a positive role model, but truth will always remain truth, and some individuals will recognise it and want to practise it because it is the truth.

Multiculturalism and gender

Working on development issues does not only mean that one must address issues of culture within developing countries: it is also necessary to address multiculturalism. As a Southern person working for a Northern Funding Agency, multicultural-ism to me means being able to adjust to a particular culture without sacrificing my own beliefs. It demands respect for other people's dignity, while remaining confident about one's own beliefs and ways of behaving. Multiculturalism is taken into account in popular education, because it recognises the differences in every community and respects the differences through showing that there is always a reason behind why people do what they do; changing beliefs and atti-tudes can come through sharing and exchanging ideas.

Northern agencies have a culture of their own which has developed over years of experience in their own base countries as well as experiences from the various countries in which they work. This culture may not be understood by communities and perhaps even by staff working for the Northern agency.

Development is about relationships, and relationships are give and take. Sometimes one has to bend rules and regulations in order to create the relationship without compromising principles. This is difficult as it involves use of personal judgement in delicate personal matters, especially when working on gender. How do you approach the disadvantaged, and ensure that you facilitate rather than dictate or direct what they should do? It involves knowing the community, its language, its customs and traditions; and being able to establish with that community which of its customs and traditions are negative, while reinforcing the positive beliefs.

It is important to respect the ways of working of communities themselves. Generally, people in Southern Africa take time to express themselves, and time to trust development workers. The slow building-up of trust is often the key to social change.

Conclusion

I have given simple examples here of ways in which we can challenge the oppressive aspects of culture, which may sound too basic; yet, for most development work this is the level at which we are working. Talking about gender in theoretical terms will only achieve so much: more can be done by creating role models which give women a positive image, in the eyes of both men and women. Custom and tradition play an indispensable part in our lives, since individuals cannot depend on themselves alone to track their way through life; yet, if traditions have outlived their usefulness and begun to pull us backwards, we must feel free to challenge them.

The current global economic crisis presents opportunities for NGOs who are working on gender issues. In addition to making financial and human resources available, and respecting other ways of working, there is need for NGOs to engage in vigorous advocacy and lobbying work to challenge women's subordination worldwide.

JOHN BARRACLOUGH/OXFAM

Colleta Chitsike is Project Co-ordinator for Oxfam in Zimbabwe.

Changes towards an increased importance for women in income generation and other developments in the socio-economic sphere need to be harnessed in a creative way, with the realisation that real and valuable change occurs over a long period of time. Challenging culture always takes time and runs the risk of causing trauma.

In addition to popular education and strong female role models, a positive image of women can be reinforced by other means, through the media and in school, in gender-aware health programmes with an emphasis on community development, in government and quasi-government training institutions, and in all other educational institutions, whether run by churches, or various different types of NGOs. All elements in this multi-faceted approach are needed, in order to have an impact on challenging culture and promoting social change.

Challenging cultural constraints

a personal testimony

DISHA is one of the oldest-established Oxfam project partners in Uttah Pradesh, India. One woman tells Liz Clayton how her involvement in work for DISHA became a catalyst for her to challenge purdah and dress restrictions in her community, and ultimately to change attitudes to women in her family and wider society.

For the last ten years, DISHA has been working with rural women and Baan (rope-making) workers. It has been successful in encouraging village level women's organisations to undertake various income-generating activities and to fight aspects of culture which work against women's empowerment. It provides legal support and education, counselling centres, and mother and child health care. In mid-1993, some of the women's organisations supported by DISHA made history by staging a demonstration against liquor licensing. Their success and steadfastness became national and international news.

Challenging cultural constraints which prevent women benefiting from development cannot happen in isolation from a practical intervention, whether this is through income-generation or through gender training. All practical interventions have an effect on gender relations, and therefore have a potential to empower or further disempower women. Through DISHA's commitment to working with women, traditions which curtail their freedom and autonomy are challenged.

Rehana Khatun Adeer's story

I was a housewife, and as a member of a Muslim family I had no freedom to come out of my house. We accept that we cannot do anything without the support of our men. But they must also recognise that they cannot do anything without us. Husband and wife should be friends. But at the moment, those words — husband, wife — indicate tension and imbalance.

As my father was a teacher, I had some education. But my father had problems; my mother died; he remarried, and I didn't get on with his new wife; otherwise he would not have made me marry so young. I was married at 13, and I faced the sort of problems in my in-laws' house that all Indian women, and particularly Muslim women, face.

I wasn't shown any affection in my husband's home; and then to make matters worse, when I started having children, I had three girls one after the other. This didn't help my position in the family or the community. Each time I was pregnant I was worried about what would happen.

Eventually I had five daughters, and they became the cause of dispute within the family. Other family members threatened that my husband would divorce me and marry another woman, to have sons. Even the other women in the household would say it. My husband said nothing; but after our third daughter was born he took to drinking, and that made life difficult, as you can imagine — a poor family with someone spending money on alcohol!

Anyway, after my first three daughters were born, I had a severe attack of typhoid. Soon afterwards, my father met me at a family wedding and was shocked at my appearance and the state of my health, and asked me to come home. So I did: I went back to my father's house. My father was very angry with my in-laws and their treatment of me, and told them that he would not send me back until they changed their ways. I had also decided that I wouldn't go back to live in their house, no matter what, and when my husband arrived to take me back I refused to go. He asked me who would support me and my three children, and I told him that my family would.

At the time my father was still teaching. Even so, I was under pressure as my brothers and their wives weren't very happy at my presence — but it was still better than at my in-laws' house. But I could only stay because I had my father's support.

After a while, my husband also came to live with us in my father's house. My father managed to persuade him to give up drinking, by promising to find him a good job. My husband was a skilled foundry worker, and my father found him a job at a foundry in Saharanpur. As my husband was responsible for selling the tools the foundry made, he established good relationships in the markets. Then we started a small foundry in Sultanpur; my father invested in the business; and I started working with my husband. I used

to get up early to light the furnace, and through our joint efforts we started earning a reasonable income. Gradually my husband stopped drinking — thanks to my father's love he lost all his bad habits. And as he changed, I got the power to live.

Starting work for DISHA

Before the Mahila Samakya programme started in 1989, I hadn't had any direct relationship with DISHA. I was aware that there was a social organisation, and I knew Tiwari-ji, the co-ordinator of DISHA, by sight; we exchanged greetings if we saw each other in the market.

At this time I used to wear a *bourkha* (a long garment which can cover the face as well as the body), and, whenever I went to the market, I would wear it. Then one day I met Tiwari-ji, and he said: 'Why don't you join us?' I said, 'I have small children, and I wear a *bourkha* — how can I work?' But he persuaded me that I could do it, that it wasn't like a government job, and that in this job I would learn as well as teach. I didn't commit myself, but when DISHA began selecting women for the Mahila Samakya programme, Tiwari-ji came to my house to ask me again.

Even then I wasn't ready to 'come out of my house'. I had a heavy heart, thinking about everything I had to do at home — the cleaning, looking after the children — but my father convinced me that I should join. Then there were various tests to do, and we had to write a letter about our life and experiences. Mine was selected as the best. Then they offered me a job. Even then I was quite unsure. But I said yes anyway.

Challenging traditional dress restrictions

Our initial task was to do a survey. So for the first time I started going out to villages. To start with I wore my *bourkha*, but I felt that I couldn't work in it; so I discussed it with my father. He just said, 'Well, leave it off then!' I was frightened about asking my husband, but eventually he too agreed.

Muslim women wearing bourkhas, northern India.

So, I threw away my *bourkha*, and went out without it. There are big villages of Muslims in our area, and from my name people realised that I too was a Muslim. One day, in the village of Dhabedkala, I met an old Muslim man who said: 'Your name is Rehana, and you are a Muslim, how much money do you want? I will give you any amount of money if you will tell your father to get you married.' I was very angry — but also embarrassed, and told him that I was married, and that I had three children. When he heard that, he said: 'Who is the bloody fool Muslim who has left his wife like this — roaming the village like a cheap woman? No proper Muslim family can send their women out like this. The men of your family must be impotent to send their wives out like this.'

Well, this incident frightened me, and I was worried that it might create communal tension in the area, so I just kept quiet. When I got home I told my father. He said: 'You should have told him that your father was competent enough to get you married, and that the decision to 'come out' was your own — not to dance or do a cabaret, but for the well-being of society. You tell him that!' So I did. The next time I went to the village I told him: 'I am working for society. If you see me doing wrong, *then* you can criticise me.' The old man is dead now; but eventually he understood what we are trying to do, and even praised our efforts.

In Sultanpur a Muslim priest opposed me. He came and told my father that he shouldn't be sending his daughter out like this, saying: 'Do you know where bloody Tiwari is? Why is he collecting women? They may be converting them to Hindus or Christians; already they are asking them to take off their *bourkhas*.' He was, for a while, my biggest opponent in Sultanpur. Now he comes to me for advice over even tiny problems. And when he has to go and see government officials he takes me. So things have changed — but only after a long struggle.

The first time I went to my in-laws' house without my *bourkha*, I could hardly walk, I was so nervous. I didn't know what would happen; but my husband said: 'You have made your decision, so come, don't worry.' So I went, like a guilty person — my face was red, my legs were shaking. They said I was shameless. But after three or four visits, they gave up.

When they heard I was going out to work, my in-laws made a big fuss. They started nagging my husband, saying things like: 'You're eating the earnings of your wife.' He faced a lot of humiliation, even within the community, but I persuaded him that he should still support me.

I have taken all these steps gradually, after much thought, and much discussion with my father and husband. And after five daughters I was facing a different struggle at home; I used to feel responsible for having no sons. Soon after I joined DISHA, I became pregnant for the sixth time. I wanted to have an abortion, but there was a huge fuss in the community. I told them, 'It will be another girl, so I will have an abortion.' Then, all my family said, 'Let what happens happen; if it is another girl then we will accept it, but don't get rid of this child.' I realised that as I had taken up, and won, the issue of the *bourkha*, that I had to compromise somewhere, so I accepted it. And when I gave birth to my sixth child — it was a boy! Suddenly they all began looking after me! As if all those girls had been my fault.

Effects of the project

My involvement with DISHA has changed my relationship with my family. Although I am still not totally free, my life is much better than before. People who once opposed me have seen my work and become silent, or have begun praising my work. In my own family, my two younger sisters also work with DISHA, and have also given up the *bourkha*. My youngest sister told her husband that she wouldn't marry him if he was going to insist that she wore a *bourkha*! My middle sister's marriage was all arranged, but when the family heard that she wouldn't wear a *bourkha*, and that she went out to work, they said their son wouldn't marry her unless she gave up work, and wore the *bourkha*. Our whole family agreed to cancel the marriage.

In my in-laws' household, no-one was educated, but now all the daughters are getting a proper education. My eldest daughter is in standard 10, and none of my daughters wears a *bourkha* — none of them will — this I won't compromise on. I tell them that it is better to stay single than wear the *bourkha*. I can prepare my

Rehana Khatun Adeer (centre, arms folded) taking part in a DISHA meeting.

daughters, but they will have to struggle for these causes.

The attitudes of people in my community have changed as well, now DISHA is well established, and people know more about it, and more about why we go out to the villages. Many women in my neighbourhood have stopped wearing the *bourkha*. The Mosque used to boycott us; they even forbade me to read the Koran. In the early days there was a lot of opposition, but now they have said everything they can say, and they are seeing that the women they are abusing are actually progressing at home and on the social front.

Whenever my neighbours are in need of help, I help them; if children need to be immunised or a baby delivered, I'll support them; I'll take them to hospital and even stay with them if necessary. Most of them now support us, but there is still some opposition. The difference is that whereas five years ago everyone was against us, now only half are! And I hope that they, too, will change their minds. But criticism and opposition are good for us: they give us strength.

Building awareness

Without organisation we are nothing. The organisation gives us power. Now I can fight any struggle. The first priority in empowering women to challenge their oppression is making them aware of the problem. Once they are aware, they can see the sense of education. Without awareness, education is useless. Many women are graduates, but they are not aware of their rights — so what good was their education? DISHA's women workers are literate, and are much more aware about society. The women who have learned how to read and write in our classes are more aware than highly educated women. They know, for example, which government department to approach to have drinking water installed; how the village committee functions; how to get a loan from the bank; and most importantly, they know how to fight for their rights.

The first priority in empowering women to challenge their oppression is making them aware of the problem.

I never imagined the world I live in now. Before I joined DISHA, I felt about a hundred years old — I was just marking time. Now, I want to live for a hundred years so I can work for the uplift of women. My economic situation is good. I'm not rich, but I am earning, and that improves my status and power within my family. Now I can speak up in a strong voice when there are things that I object to.

I want to live as a good person, and I want to do something for those women who are still exploited and harassed by their own families. Still women are beaten; still women are raped; and that reminds me of my own struggle. If I had not had support from my family and from DISHA I couldn't have got here. I want to provide the same kind of support to women in our area — to assist them is my ambition. I want to take them out of purdah, and out from the *bourkha* — as a Muslim women, that is my first duty.

I want us to organise women, and get the support of everyone, as well as enough resources for our programme, so that we can create the world of our dreams as soon as possible. A world where all women can say: 'This is *my* property; this is *my* house; these are *my* children.' Where all people will be equal: men and women.

Rehana Khatun Adeer was interviewed by Liz Clayton of Oxfam's Resources Unit.

Working with a radical agenda

the Musasa project, Zimbabwe

Sheelagh Stewart

The Musasa Project, a Zimbabwean NGO, was set up in 1988 to deal with the problem of violence against women. This article looks at how and why the Musasa Project has adopted an increasingly radical agenda for cultural change in Zimbabwe: an agenda which challenges existing values, and represents an alternative in its own society.

There are no definitive figures on the extent of domestic violence against women in Zimbabwe, but interviewees in the initial nine-month pilot project (Taylor and Stewart, 1989) estimated that domestic violence affected between 50 per cent and 80 per cent of all partnerships. Interviews and training exercises with the Zimbabwe Republic Police (ZRP) confirmed initial impressions that, not only was violence against women widespread, but it was also acceptable within the society at large.

The attitude that violence against women is acceptable is one which is shared with many other countries in the world. In Zimbabwe, however, this attitude is exacerbated by aspects of culture and tradition, such as the bridewealth system (*lobola*) which by 'selling' women to their future husbands, reinforces the impression that the woman is the husband's property, to do with as he wishes, beating her included. (For a fuller explanation of *lobola* and its relationship to the position of women in Zimbabwe, and particularly to the incidence of domestic violence, see Stewart, 1992.) There are a number of sayings within Zimbabwean culture which condone domestic violence. It is often said, for example, that 'beating one's wife is a sign of love'.

In a context such as this the establishment of the Musasa Project is in itself a radical initiative. Further, an early decision was made by the project to deal with the issue by tackling the roots of the problem. Instead of dealing only with women who were victims and survivors of domestic violence, through establishing shelters and providing counselling, Musasa sought to transform the society through an extensive public education campaign.

It is clear from initiatives conducted around the world (Schuler, M. (ed); 1982) that there are two principal reasons for the prevalence of violence against women, particularly domestic violence: the first is the widespread existence of attitudes condoning such violence; and the second is the duplication of these attitudes within agencies whose responsibility it is to prevent such abuse of human rights, for example, the police and the legal system. If these are the root causes, then shelters for battered women, though invaluable for the individuals concerned, do nothing to tackle the underlying causes of violence against women.

While the work of the Musasa Project aims primarily to address root causes, this does not mean that Musasa has not also addressed the needs of individuals who have suffered domestic violence, through counselling and practical assistance. Since the inception of the project, emotional and practical support has been provided to increasing numbers of women (Njovana, 1994).

Early experience in the project indicated that, in addition to being of value to the individuals concerned, ongoing contact and work with the survivors of violence, broader educational initiatives, and legal strategies, were targeted at the causes of violence inherent within Zimbabwean society. Cost-effective strategies were developed, which worked for individual survivors. Although this 'radical' approach fits well into current trends and thinking about the importance of 'participatory development', it was not generally accepted by donors in 1988. The counselling element of the project was exceptionally difficult to fund, with some donors refusing point blank to consider this item of expenditure, while others, though not approving, were prepared to fund the project with 'no strings attached'. The 'no strings' money was used to fund the counselling element of the project.

This combining of individual concerns with broader-based development work has continued with the recent employment of a legal practitioner, who provides both practical legal support for survivors of domestic violence, but also works for change within the legal system.

Educating the ZRP: the roots of a radical agenda?

The starting point for Musasa's public education programme was work with the Zimbabwe Republic Police (ZRP). The project began with the Police Community Relations Liaison Officers (CRLO), and progressed to education work with other branches of the police, with a programme for constables at police station level, since this is the first port of call for survivors of domestic violence. The work with the police was modelled on Freirian principles of public education, and always started by the identification, together with the police, of the problems they experienced in dealing with violence against women. After the police had identified a number of problems, they were then invited to suggest solutions. The Musasa Project, and other agencies where appropriate, then worked with the police on these solutions.

A good example of this process involved the identification by the police as a problem the fact that women who laid charges of domestic violence often withdrew the charges. The ZRP, in common with police all over the world, are judged on their crime clear-up rates, and were therefore unsympathetic, if they judged that they might invest time and effort in a case where the charges were likely to be withdrawn. Musasa invited police to consider in a workshop setting why the charges might be withdrawn. As a result of this, all rape and domestic violence survivors are now interviewed in private in the police station, treated sympathetically, and encouraged to lay charges. The combination of different treatment from the police and the support where possible of the Musasa Project, has meant that the number of cases reported and prosecuted has increased (Njovana, 1994).

This example raises another problem experienced by the police. They found their interaction with the government legal

Participants in a training course for community workers in Zimbabwe. Role–play can be a useful technique for exploring the issue of domestic violence.

service frustrating, sometimes because cases which they had worked hard on were badly prosecuted, and sometimes because the backlog in the legal system (up to three years between crime and prosecution in some instances) meant that results of the investigative work seemed remote from the work itself. Once again, this opened the door for further innovative work, this time with the legal system. The police hosted, and continue to host, a series of one-day workshops with the legal services, facilitated by the Musasa Project. During these workshops, problems experienced in communication and operations between the police and legal services were aired. A number of extremely fruitful debates between the police and legal services about the issue were held, and problem areas and potential solutions, such as rapid prosecution of domestic violence cases, suggested.

In the context of Zimbabwean society, and the domestic violence issue, the work of the Musasa Project was both radical and innovative. The project's statements to the outside world have progressed to more and bolder statements about Zimbabwean society.

Starting slowly: introducing a radical agenda

Despite the clear decision to tackle the roots of the problem, Musasa was careful about directly tackling social mores, such as the belief that the man is the head of the house, and the practice of bridewealth. The project began with a clear statement of non-identification with feminism of any variety. It was also extremely cautious about how it presented both itself and the problem of domestic violence. The overall image presented by the project of itself, was that of a 'helping' agency, set up to give assistance to victims of domestic violence.

When asked about the causes of domestic violence, project members spoke of stress caused by economic difficulties, and the breakdown of the traditional family, caused in some cases by increasing urbanisation. The traditional authority of men, as household heads, to beat their wives, was questioned. A 'Real Men Don't Beat Their Wives' campaign was launched. Other campaigns, such as 'Domestic Violence is Bad for Our Nation', also mark this phase of the project.

The project was allowed a surprising amount of freedom during this phase. There was extensive press and television coverage of the project and what it was trying to achieve, and a number of high-ranking government officials made statements in support of the Musasa Project and against domestic violence. The relationship with the ZRP was consolidated and strengthened. At the end of the first three years, the project was secure, both financially, and within Zimbabwean society. Strong contacts had been made with relevant ministry officials, the legal services and with the police. At this point there was a change in leadership and the founders of the project, Jill Taylor and I, withdrew from the project, as per the original project plan (Stewart and Taylor, 1988). The project has been marked since then by an increasing radicalisation of both its programme and public image.

The project now addresses gender issues directly through a series of gender workshops, which aim to make all elements of Zimbabwean society aware of 'how patriarchy works within all structures of our society' (Musasa, Annual report 1993-94). In addition, the project is now addressing broader issues of the position of women in society. An example is the position taken by the project on the land issue in Zimbabwe:

Musasa has been taking a more active role in addressing issues which may not appear directly related to acts of domestic violence, but in fact can partly be the underlying causes of battering. For example the land issue in Zimbabwe is a hot, current, controversial topic. Women must have the right to own land and have equal access to land acquisition. A woman's dependence on a man can intensify her vulnerability and leave her with less options if he is battering her.

Perhaps the most interesting tradition associated with women's subordination is that of *lobola*. During the early years of the project, *lobola* was hardly mentioned in connection with domestic violence, except to comment that the commercialisation and consequent high cost of *lobola* had exacerbated economic stress and therefore indirectly affected the problem of domestic violence. Musasa's legal practitioner, Rudo Mhungu, commented recently, that

... lobola has become instrumental in controlling and battering women. lobola is not only used by men to oppress women, but also by society as a whole. Women become devalued when lobola is paid for them because they are reduced to the equivalent of a commodity ... Once lobola is paid for the woman, her child bearing capacity and earning ability are entirely owned by the husband ... This aids in creating the harmful belief that beating a woman is within a husband's rights since he has paid for her. (Binks, 1994.)

This statement poses a radical, bold, and confident challenge to the system of male privilege in Zimbabwe. It is also a good example of the increasing assertiveness of the Musasa Project in the Zimbabwean context.

Why this shift in tactics?

Finally, this paper will ponder possible reasons for this shift in operating tactics towards an explicitly feminist agenda. I would suggest that the first reason is connected with the established nature of the organisation, its increasing membership, and secure funding base (Musasa Annual Report, 1993-94). It would appear that this has given the organisation confidence to start addressing some of the more sensitive and difficult issues within Zimbabwean society and to pose some direct challenges to male power and dominance.

The other possible reason is less obvious, but a brief discussion of it may throw interesting light on the role of outsiders in connection with issues such as domestic violence in the developing world. The project was founded by two white Zimbabweans, Jill Taylor and Sheelagh Stewart. In terms of the first project plan, their role was to be temporary, until the organisation was established, whereupon they would withdraw. Nine months were spent looking for a model which was appropriate for Zimbabwe, the project was established, and within three years the leadership passed into the hands of black Zimbabweans. The role of anti-racist white Africans in post-colonialist Africa is awkward (but possibly not less awkward than the role of whites from previously colonial powers). We are neither outsiders nor insiders in the true sense. In terms of a project like the Musasa Project, this meant that we were extremely careful about what we criticised. This caution in the leadership was responsible at least in part for the cautious approach to issues such as *lobola* and the carefully presented image of the Musasa Project as a 'helping' organisation. This caution was probably appropriate, both in terms of the needs of the organisation at its inception and in terms of the ambiguous position of white Zimbabwean criticism of black Zimbabwean culture.

Ambivalence is by definition two-sided. The other side to our ambivalent position is that as 'quasi-outsiders', especially as female quasi-outsiders, we were allowed far more freedom of movement than black Zimbabwean women. This is both literal, in terms of safety on the streets, and cultural, in terms of being able to say and do things which it would be unacceptable for black Zimbabwean women to say and do. It is possible, therefore, that a role for outsiders in such a context may be to start the ball rolling and create the space for a truly indigenous organisation, which can in due course take a more radical role in its own society. It is equally possible that this statement is presumptuous, and that any initiative on violence against women, would have ended up being radical in this way. What remains true, at the end of the day, is that the liberation of women from their own oppressive cultural constraints has to be undertaken by the women of that culture by themselves.

Sheelagh Stewart comes from Zimbabwe. From 1988 to 1991, she was Co-ordinator/Director and Consultant to the Musasa Project, and is now completing a PhD at the Institute of Development Studies, University of Sussex, UK.

Bibliography

Armstrong, A and Ncube, W (1987) *Women and Law in Southern Africa*, Harare, Zimbabwe Publishing House.

Binks, M (1994) 'Limitations of the human rights framework', *Claiming Our Place: Working the Human Rights System to Women's Advantage*, Washington, Institute for Women, Law and Development.

Chirume, L (1989) *A Study of the Phenomenon of Wife Beating: Zimbabwe as a Case Study*, University of Zimbabwe.

Cotton, A (1993) 'Proposal for Funding the Cambridge Female Education Trust: Educating Girls to Secondary School Level in Zimbabwe', unpublished ms.

MATCH (1993) 'End to Violence Against Women: African Women's Initiatives', End to Violence Against Women: Africa

Women's Initiatives, ZESA Training Centre, Harare, Zimbabwe, Musasa Project.

Meursing, C et al (1993) *Child Sexual Abuse in Matabeleland*, Matabeleland Aids Council.

Musasa (1993-94) *The Musasa Project, Sixth Annual Report*, The Musasa Project.

Njovana, E (1994) 'Gender-based violence and sexual assault', *African Women* 8: 17.

Runganga, A (1990) *The use of herbal and non-herbal agents in sexualintercourse by a sample of Zimbabwean women*, University of Zimbabwe.

Rwezaura, B (1985) *Traditional Family Law and Change in Tanzania: A Study of the Kuria Social System*, Baden-Baden, Nomos Verlagsgesellschaft.

Schuler, M (ed.) (1982) *Freedom from Violence. Women's Strategies from around the World*, New York, UNIFEM.

ILLUSTRATION: COLLEEN CRAWFORD COUSINS

A page from a training manual produced by the Musasa Project.

Women, conflict, and culture in former Yugoslavia

Jovanka Stojsavljevic

Conflict signals a shock to the social order; violence against women escalates in the absence of cultural controls, and may be used as a weapon of war, and as a propaganda tool. This article examines these issues in the context of former Yugoslavia, and discusses women's resistance to nationalist agendas.

The countries of Slovenia, Yugoslavia (Serbia and Montenegro), Croatia, Bosnia, and Macedonia have had an extremely turbulent history. As a result, the women's movement in the region has undergone many changes. In some circumstances, it has succumbed or adapted to the dominant culture and the political line taken by the government of the day. At other times, the movement has opposed the regime.

Since the break-up of former Yugoslavia, elements of these different reactions have taken place side by side. It has been tragic to witness women and women's groups, who were once united on the principles of global rights for women, becoming fragmented across the lines of the nationalist agendas of the warring parties. At the same time, it is incredible to see so many women continuing to resist the nationalist agenda, and to defy the state-controlled media propaganda. For three years, women's groups have organised to support survivors of war. They have raised funds to buy safe houses. They have worked relentlessly, without salaries. Against all odds, women refuse to hate their fellow people on the grounds of their ethnic identity, even though they and their families have now been suffering war for three years.

The women's movement in former Yugoslavia

Tragically, one of the first events that took place at the onset of the war was the disintegration of the women's movement across male-defined nationalist boundaries. In 1987, the first National Feminist Conference of Yugoslavia was held in Ljubljana. One of the resolutions of this conference was that women would not recognise artificial male boundaries; that they were united in sisterhood, and their common experiences as women over-rode male concerns for territorial rights and geographical boundaries. It was also resolved that the male power struggles should not be enacted across women's bodies. These resolutions have been challenged by the current civil war.

The women's movement in Yugoslavia was born during the Second World War, with the formation of the Anti-Fascist Front of Women. With the aim of ridding the territory of fascism, women fought alongside their male compatriots on the front line, against the German Nazis, the Chetniks of Serbia, who were mainly royalists and supporters of the Orthodox Church, and the Ustashi, fascists who were backed by Hitler and formed a puppet state. In effect, Yugoslavia suffered a civil war while the world warred around it. As is the case today, many unlikely alliances between women were formed across the territory, as factions who were normally opposed joined in co-operation to attack the 'other side'.

After the success of the 'partisans' in suppressing the fascists, and the establishment of the Socialist Federal Republics of Yugoslavia, the Anti-Fascist Front of Women was disbanded by the Communist Party, on the basis that, under communism, women would have equal rights with men, and so there was no need to organise separately. However, communism has never effectively addressed the fact that societies throughout the world are patriarchal, regardless of their political and economic structures. This means that there are a number of unwritten rules and regulations, implicit to our cultures, that explicitly disadvantage women.

In the 1970s, Yugoslavia witnessed the setting-up of groups of women intellectuals, who discussed and analysed the role of women in society. These groups were not involved in any kind of advocacy for women's rights, nor were they involved in supporting women whose rights had been abused. In the early 1980s, a movement of feminist activists emerged, influenced by the women's peace movement in the West; they organised fairly independently, often in opposition to state institutions. These feminist groups became actively involved in advocacy and support work on issues affecting women's lives, including rape and domestic violence, pornography, and women's right to employment. The first SOS telephone-helpline for women and children experiencing rape and domestic violence was established in 1986, in Zagreb. Soon afterwards, a refuge for abused women was established.

The present situation

The women's movement in former Yugoslavia has been deeply affected by the nationalist agenda; it has lost the power to articulate any effective and united opposition to the war, and has so far been unable to prevent the widespread use of the violation of women as a propaganda tool to promote a nationalist agenda.

The language of the women's movement is now being used to further nationalist agendas: a leading member of the nationalist faction of the Croatian women's movement is quoted as making a comparison between Serb/male/aggression against Croatia as a woman's body that is being assaulted. This statement caused a crisis which has led to Croatian feminists refusing to share platforms with Serbian feminists at international gatherings of women opposed to the war, and attacks on feminists from Europe and America who invited women from Belgrade to such meetings.

In both Serbia and Croatia, those feminists who have refused to embrace the resurgence of nationalism and patriotism are accused of being enemies of the State by nationalist feminists, and by the mainstream media. Some have had to take refuge in other countries.

The feminist movement in Serbia has been further demoralised by the collective guilt feminists feel for the actions of the Serbian/Yugoslavian army and the Yugoslavian government. The war in former Yugoslavia first broke out in Slovenia, in June 1991, lasting for ten days.

In Croatia, it broke out in August 1991. Even at this stage, people in Bosnia vociferously stressed that it could never break out there. While Yugoslavia disintegrated, political leaders in Bosnia — Karadzic, Izetbegovic and Kljuic — were talking of running a collective presidency representing a multicultural society! War finally came to Bosnia in May 1992.

The war in former Yugoslavia is rooted in an attempt by old guard communists to use the ideology of nationalism to shore up their personal power. The first overtly public signs of this nationalism came in a speech by Slobodan Milosevic, leader of the Serbs, in 1989, in which he called on all Serbs to commemorate the battle of Kosovo and remember that this was the heart of their kingdom, before Ottoman occupation; he asserted that Serbs should never allow themselves to be oppressed again. This speech preceded a violent oppression of the Kosovo miners' strike, and the introduction of what is now effectively military rule.

Women are seen as guardians of their culture; sexual insults may be used if they threaten political agendas which are set by men. During 1987, the year that Milosevic became leader of the Serb Communist Party, and liberals were removed from influential positions, Ali Sukrija, leader of the Communist Party of Kosovo, was quoted as saying 'Serbian women in Kosovo were only fit to be prostitutes in cafes'. Serbian women in Kosovo staged spontaneous demonstrations, calling for intervention from the Yugoslav army to protect them from abuse. Demonstrators carried placards saying: 'We gave up our sons for Yugoslavia, now the Yugoslavian army should protect us!'

In 1990 the constitution of Serbia was changed. Kosovo and Vojvodina were no longer independent provinces of Serbia, except on paper, and the heads of the local communist parties were changed to those who were pro-Milosevic. At the Fourteenth Congress of Yugoslav Communists, Slovenians, and Croats walked out as Milosevic sought to gain control of the Yugoslav Communist Party.

Soon after the outbreak of war, women's groups were organised by the respective governments, in order to ensure that nationalist views were articulated to, and by, women. Thus, while women demonstrated against their sons being drafted into the Yugoslavian army, the same groups kept quiet when men were mobilised into the newly formed Serbian, Croatian or Bosnian armies. Those women who did oppose the conscription of their sons into their own national armies were vilified and accused of wanting the destruction of their own people, by not wanting the country to defend itself.

Women's resistance to nationalism

Some excellent work has been carried out by women's groups who refused the nationalist agenda, and many new initiatives have been developed, since the onset of war. There are now literally hundreds of NGOs in former Yugoslavia; many of them are women's groups, set up for many different reasons. However, an aim common to all of them is to provide support to women and children who have suffered sexual violence, 'ethnic cleansing', the separation from, or death of, their loved ones, and the loss of their homes and livelihoods. Women and children form approximately 80 per cent of the displaced population across the territory of former Yugoslavia.

Some women's groups have maintained a strong political focus for their work, despite ridicule and attack. The group known as Women in Black, based in Belgrade, organises weekly demonstrations against the war; members stand in the city's central square, dressed in black, in silent protest against the war.

Bosnian refugee in Croatia. In former Yugoslavia, violence against women is publicised for propaganda purposes; the newspaper headline reads 'Through terror to greater Serbia'

Women, war, and sexual violence

Throughout history, sexual attacks on women have formed a common strategy of male warfare. The aim of this strategy is to humiliate enemy men, and destroy the fabric of the family and society; a raped woman is no longer viewed as 'clean', and often no longer has a place in her family or community. This view is clearly expressed in an article in one national newspaper in Serbia, describing a woman's experience of rape by the enemy. The article ended, 'She would be better off dead than alive to shame her husband, her family and her community by giving birth to a child from the seed of the enemy.'

Raping and impregnating women also serves as a strategy of 'ethnic cleansing': if a man from one nationality makes a woman from the enemy nationality pregnant, then the child will automatically take on the nationality of the rapist. In the old patriarchal tradition, it is the father's nationality that is important, and defines the nationality of the child.

In a collective centre in Croatia, where refugees and displaced people are housed, a refugee woman was forced to flee again after other refugees found out that she had been raped, and would not get an abortion. Ironically, this is in a country where the Catholic church has a very strong influence, and where the government had attempted, unsuccessfully, to introduce legislation against abortion.

Despite the widespread incidence of rape in conflict throughout history, this has tended not to be recorded, except where it can be used for propaganda purposes. The war in former Yugoslavia has highlighted rape as a strategy of war, and this has as a result placed rape, occurring in the context of conflict, on the international agenda. However, at the height of the war in

Somalia, women in that country were also being used and abused in their own civil war, but this received no public attention.

The international community has work to do if rape is to be recognised fully as a human rights issue. Rape of women is not even mentioned in the Geneva Conventions; and women seeking asylum in Britain, on the basis of gender-based persecution, are often rejected on the grounds that being raped is a side-consequence of war, arbitrarily meted out, and so does not amount to 'persecution on the grounds of political beliefs'.

The reason why the issue of rape now has a public profile in former Yugoslavia is only because of its use as a weapon of propaganda.

It could be argued that the reason why the issue of rape now has a public profile in former Yugoslavia is only because of its use as a weapon of propaganda; it suits a number of political agendas, which concern both the national and international communities: namely, geographical boundaries, territorial rights, and sovereign states. It seems that it is not the right of women to protection from sexual violation that is important, but the wider political battles that can be fought through their experience of violation.

The use of rape in conflict to further these agendas results in further violations of a woman's dignity and integrity. She merely becomes the victim or object of her own experience; her rape is seen as important only because it is committed by a man or men from an alien ethnic group, and not because rape is a crime of violence against her.

Publicity about rape in former Yugoslavia has resulted in further insensitivities, or even outright abuse, being aimed at women who have experienced rape. NGOs and journalists have flooded into the territory, saying 'I want to interview a raped woman', or 'I want to counsel women who have been raped.' Books have been written with gratuitous details of women's experiences of rape. I would ask why this is; surely it is not to improve care and support for the victims of rape, nor to advocate women's rights during war, but rather to prove that one race of men is the aggressor against another race of men. Invariably, sensational media coverage of the rape of women in former Yugoslavia has resulted in women rape victims becoming unable to voice their trauma; this additional torment for women who have already undergone extreme suffering has attracted condemnation from indigenous women's groups across the territory.

Women's survival strategies

The suffering caused to women by the war is not limited to rape, 'ethnic cleansing', loss of homes, livelihoods, family and friends. War causes the destruction of economies and the social welfare system. As a result, women are forced to become single heads of their families and take responsibility for provision of food, clothes, and other necessities, as well as caring for vulnerable members: children, the elderly, and the disabled.

One of Oxfam's strategic aims in former Yugoslavia is 'to empower women to challenge the causes and alleviate the effects of gender-based suffering caused by patriarchal structuring of society and exacerbated by armed conflict'. Fundamental to this aim is that women's voices are heard; that women articulate their own experiences and needs, and formulate their own strategies for survival. Oxfam is currently working on an initiative to record women's testimonies of war. It is a contribution towards ensuring that women's voices are heard from their own perspec-

BILL STEPHENSON/OXFAM

An income–generating project can provide an opportunity for women who have experienced violence to support each other.

tive as subjects of their experience and as a force for change.

A number of other initiatives have been developed over the past two years to support women to reconstruct the fabric of their society. In Tuzla, we have a psycho-social programme, in the form of occupational workshops where women can meet and talk, away from the refugee centres. Here, women can utilise their skills and earn a small income, by sewing and knitting warm clothing for other refugees in central Bosnia. Oxfam is supporting a similar initiative in Belgrade.

In Croatia, Oxfam has helped to strengthen and build the capacity of a local women's group, that facilitates self-help and mutual support groups for displaced women and refugees. We are also preparing a programme that will enable displaced women who cannot return home, to achieve sustainable livelihoods through training in micro-enterprise.

Another strategy for achieving our aim is to facilitate communication and networking between women's groups across the territory of Former Yugoslavia. Apart from planning a regional conference on violence against women and enabling local partners to participate in the UN conference on Women in Beijing, Oxfam has funded Electronic Witches to link up Oxfam offices and various women's groups to E-mail. This will ensure that groups who are currently isolated, will be able to make contact, share information, experience and knowledge with other groups working on similar issues, both across the territory and internationally.

Jovanka Stojsavljevic is Oxfam's Regional Representative for former Yugoslavia.

The rise of religious fundamentalism in Britain

the experience of Women Against Fundamentalism

Sue Katz

Women Against Fundamentalism (WAF) was launched on 6 May 1989 to challenge the rise of fundamentalism in all religions. By fundamentalism we do not mean religious observance, which we see as a matter of individual choice, but rather modern political movements, which we assert use religion as a basis for their attempt to win or consolidate power and extend social control.

Fundamentalism appears in different and changing forms in religions throughout the world, sometimes as a state project, sometimes in opposition to the state. But at the heart of all fundamentalist agendas is the control of women's minds and bodies. All religious fundamentalists support the patriarchal family as a central agent of such control. They view women as embodying the morals and traditional values of the family and the whole community.

WAF works against the increasing control that fundamentalism imposes on all our lives. We are a group of women from across the world and from a wide range of backgrounds, who are involved in many different political campaigns. We take up issues such as women's reproductive rights, and fight both to safeguard and extend abortion rights, and to resist enforced sterilisation. We struggle against religious dogma, no matter what source this comes from, which denies us our right to determine our own sexuality, and justifies violence against women.

Christian fundamentalism

Christianity is playing an increasingly central role in the redefining of European identities and the growing nationalist movements. In Britain, Christianity is the established state religion. This formal relationship between Church and State is today being exploited to promote Christianity as an expression of the British cultural identity. This is producing new expressions of racism. We believe that resistance to racism and fundamentalism in Britain must involve a struggle for secularism, in opposition to the state's official recognition of one religion. We believe that secularism is a necessary precondition for pluralism, though it does not guarantee it. In Britain, therefore, WAF is calling for the disestablishment of the Church of England, and a repeal of the blasphemy laws. We seek a phasing-out of state funding of all religious schools, and an end to the imposition of Christianity in state schools, including Christian assemblies.

In the last year we have been campaigning for secular school education and against the compulsory 'daily act of Christian worship' in British schools. This obligation means that parents who do not want their child to join in Christian worship must formally request that their child opts out of religious assembly and teaching. Children do not have the same right to opt out themselves. This can lead to the marginalisation and alienation of children of other faiths, and those who have secular beliefs. The policy also provides justification for increasing demands for state-supported religious schools for all religions, including Islam, with serious implications for girls. WAF has been organising meetings with other interested parties, including teachers' trade unions, head teachers, education authorities, parent school-governors, and humanist associations.

The state education machinery has also removed sex education from the area of compulsory science teaching, where it was traditionally located. Sex education is now included in the range of elective subjects, which means that children are not automatically receiving instruction in safer sex. Again, parents can choose not to allow their children to attend these classes, but the young people themselves have no say,

and can be denied vital health education, which is necessary to protect their health and prevent unplanned pregnancy.

Religious minorities and fundamentalism

WAF also confronts fundamentalism with British minority religions. We challenge the assumption that minorities in this country exist as unified, internally homogeneous groups. This view assumes that women's voices are represented by the 'community leaders', and denies them an independent voice. We want to live in a country of many cultures, but reject the politics of what has come to be known as 'multiculturalism'. The multicultural consensus, forged by sections of all political parties, delivers women's futures into the hands of fundamentalist community leaders, by seeing these as representatives of the community as a whole.

Working together with a community arts group called Cultural Partnership, we have made a video entitled *Across Family Lines*. In it, five women from different religious traditions describe their personal

OXFAM

WAF have been campaigning against the compulsory daily act of worship in British schools, which they believe can lead to the marginalisation and alienation of children whose parents do not wish them to take part.

experiences of the oppression of women within their various faiths, and recount how they have escaped the confines of those religions, adapting their varied cultural heritage and experience to create new rituals to fit their own lives. WAF members are touring the country with this video, leading discussion groups when it is shown in schools and community centres.

The increased political activity of the racist right-wing, especially in the East End of London, has led WAF members to active involvement in local anti-racism movements. WAF has been among those who point out the responsibility of some of the main political parties for creating an atmosphere conducive to racism. When working together with other anti-racist groups, WAF is often the only feminist organisation involved, and so fights to bring a women's perspective to the analysis.

Making links worldwide

WAF has developed a high national and international profile. Our commitment to supporting individuals and women's organisations around the world who are struggling against fundamentalism is reflected both in our extensive networking, and in our Journal, which is full of writings by women from many countries talking about their experience of different kinds of fundamentalism. There are articles about Israel, Iran, Tibet, Sudan, Britain, South Africa, Turkey, and many other places. Women who know these societies discuss the impact on their lives of the particular types of fundamentalism which are growing there. We are in contact with organisations with a parallel agenda in many countries, and often publish their writings in our Journal.

When possible, we attend relevant international conferences. Most recently we sent WAF members to the Helsinki Citizens' Assembly in Ankara, Turkey. Together with a Turkish woman, we presented a workshop on fundamentalism and racism in Europe, focusing on the position of migrant women. WAF members also attended the NGO Forum of the International Conference on Population and Development in Cairo in September, 1994. Our attendance was funded by a Dutch agency. WAF joined an international panel to discuss the political uses of religion, ethnicity, and culture.

We also try to offer support from Britain for women struggling against fundamentalism elsewhere. We have been active in a campaign against the blasphemy laws in Bangladesh, which have resulted in a *fatwa* (death threat) against the feminist writer Taslima Nasreen. Her books have been banned, a price has been put on her head, and ultimately she has been forced to flee from Bangladesh for her safety. As Britain also has blasphemy laws, we feel a strong commitment to her struggle. WAF has been instrumental in lobbying political leaders, briefing the media, and organising petitions in the community, and has also coordinated meetings with other interested organisations in Britain.

The unique contribution of WAF to UK politics and to struggles against fundamentalism worldwide is the combination of an analysis of fundamentalism, which is undeveloped in many feminist and progressive groups, with a feminism that some anti-fundamentalist and political groups have not yet addressed. The small group of volunteer activists, who organise WAF activities, facilitates the commitment of a much larger group of WAF members, who identify with our view of the dangers to women's autonomy of the various forms of fundamentalism.

Sue Katz has been a member of WAF since 1990; she has lived in the UK, the USA, and Israel, and is familiar with the many forms of fundamentalism which exist in these countries.

Culture and the law in Islam

Women Living Under Muslim Law

The Women living Under Muslim Law Network (WLUML) was set up eight years ago, to facilitate the sharing of information, contacts, ideas, and strategies among women in the Muslim world.

It is often presumed that there exists one homogeneous Muslim world. But interaction between women from different Muslim societies has shown us that, while some similarities exist, the notion of a single, uniform Muslim world is a misconception. Muslim women have been led to believe that the only way of life possible for Muslim women is the one culturally imposed on us in each of our contexts. In fact, our different realities range from being, on the one hand, strictly closeted, isolated and voiceless within four walls, subjected to public flogging, and condemned to death for presumed adultery (which is considered a crime against the State), and forcibly given in marriage as a child; to, on the other hand, being free to take up employment as professionals and to teach at universities.

We do not mean to imply that religious freedom, national sovereignty, or even the right to follow cultural traditions, are false issues. But to us, attention to such issues cannot justify ignoring the aspirations of women in Muslim countries and communities. We believe that depriving women of dreaming of a different reality is one of the most debilitating forms of oppression it is possible to suffer.

In the time since its inception, WLUML has united women in Muslim countries across the world and stimulated them to analyse and reconceptualise the nature of their situation, and to formulate workable strategies for change, according to their own priorities, and relevant to their own specific national or community contexts..

In addition to their involvement internationally, the women who work with WLUML are intimately connected with the women's movements in their own countries, often at the national as well as grassroots level.

Culture and the law

Over the last decade, much attention in the field of women's human rights has focused on the principles of international law, as expressed in human rights treaties such as the Convention on the Elimination of All Forms of Discrimination Against Women. The strategies and arguments for legal change that have informed most of these efforts around the world are profoundly different. If the movement for human rights is to be truly international in scope, then we need to share experiences, skills, and energies to support the different local needs of women in different regional or national contexts.

For women in the vastly varied Muslim communities worldwide, the rhythms, patterns, and structure of everyday life are shaped by an intricate web of laws, rules, and customs, which are often said to be Islamic. To an extent that is dramatically different for women than for men, this body of rules regulates an individual's ability to participate in every level of social life: from decision making within the home and family, to education, employment, and public office. It shapes attitudes towards female sexuality and reproduction, towards women's roles in the family and community. In short, this web of rules measures women's 'value' as human beings.

Yet, despite the intimate connection between this body of law and the quality of women's lives, it is clear that the labelling of such laws as 'Islamic' essentially puts them beyond the reach of human rights laws. So, for example, although many Muslim countries have ratified the Women's Convention, they have typically done so with reservations that deny the applicability of provisions deemed to conflict with local or national versions of Islam or Islamic laws. At the same time, traditional human rights groups — while not hesitating to champion the political and civil rights of men in Muslim countries — have been loath to address many of the issues most critical to women, ostensibly for fear of trampling on religious freedom.

Women and the Law Project

WLUML is acutely aware that on questions of how, whether, and when to pursue legal change, those who work internationally must take their lead from women's lives, work, and struggle in their own countries. Two years ago, we started the Women And the Law Project. The Project, which had been planned as long ago as 1988, set out to chart, and simultaneously conduct action-oriented research on, law in 26 countries.

In many Muslim countries, a process of growing secularisation is currently taking place alongside a growing Islamisation of state law. The law is a pervasive and powerful force between men and women; between parents and children; between citizens and the State. The extraordinary power of law in Muslim societies stems both from its roots in Islam — where, in striking contrast to religions such as Christianity, law is central to both theology and practice — and from the evolving, highly variable, and hotly contested relationship between Islam and the State.

To an extent unknown in the West, law shapes both the private and the public discourse through which social change is perceived and understood, providing the language, categories, and tools through which such change is managed. It forms the loom on which women's fate is woven.

The Women and the Law Project grows from the conviction that, for Muslim women, the power to control their destinies ultimately will lie in their ability to master the law that shapes their lives. Comparing women's varied experiences of the trends of secularisation and Islamisation potentially provides a major focus for sharing knowledge, resources, and strategies between women within the Muslim World, and linking their efforts to international initiatives beyond the Muslim world. Research of this sort has the potential to identify opportunities for the protection of human dignity of women everywhere.

WLUML hopes that this Project will lay the essential foundation for the vindication of the human rights of women in the Muslim world. First, women need to gain an understanding of how law has, over the years, been used to constrict and contain their experience. Secondly, women must take control of the modes of thought and speech, and the techniques, through which legal change in Muslim societies may potentially take place.

Opposition to gender-sensitive development

learning to answer back

Sara Hlupekile Longwe

This article argues that the problem is not so much that policies on women's development constitute an undue interference in the politics and internal affairs of sovereign states, but rather that such policies are themselves subject to gross interference. Opposition to the policies comes from within the very bureaucracies which are charged with implementing them.

Bureaucracies all over the world have long traditions of resisting and thwarting policies which they consider to be unwise or unworkable — in other words, policies to which they themselves are ideologically opposed. In the case of development policies, resistance may originate within the bureaucracy of the development agency, or within the government bureaucracy of the Third World country. In the case of policies on women's development, both the bureaucracies of the development agency and of the Third World government are likely to be male-dominated, and patriarchal in their style, beliefs, and administrative regulations. In some cases the policies on women's equality which they are being asked to implement would, if applied to their own bureaucracies, entail radical reform and threaten the positions of the present incumbents.

Interference with new policies on women's development may stem from mere inertia within the development agency, which already has existing programmes and modes of working with Third World countries, and is unwilling or unable to make the effort to re-evaluate and re-align the programme to take account of the new policy directions on women's equality and women's development.

Even more seriously, interference — in the form of lack of action — may arise from ideological opposition to women's equality. Ideological opposition is likely to be stronger in male-dominated agencies with long patriarchal traditions of administration, and paternal approaches towards development; it is also likely to be stronger in bilateral agencies based in countries which are themselves rather behind in the process of achieving equality for women. Whether arising from mere inertia or ideological opposition, the results are the same: the new policies on women's development are left, like so many other policy initiatives, as mere documents and dust upon the shelf.

Such interference cannot, of course, be justified, even within the development agency, in terms of administrative inertia or opposition to women's equality. More sophisticated and persuasive rationalisations are needed to justify lack of action, or the diversion and watering down of the new policy. The possible rationalisations are many and varied; they are directed at the home audience whose taxes fund the development agency, and whose voice pressed for the policy on women's development; they follow the general line of argument that 'we in the agency have the actual first-hand experience of working in these Third World countries, and we know the situation there, and what is possible and practicable at this time'.

Within this general line of argument can be developed quite specific rationalisations. Below I have listed seven different examples with which I am familiar, followed in each case by my own attempts at refutation. The reader may entertain herself by adding further rationalisations, and refutations.

1 *Policies on equality for women are unnecessary because development is concerned with improving general welfare; development will automatically benefit a whole community, both women and men.*

Wrong. There is now a large literature to suggest that the failure of development projects to address the special needs of women has resulted in more than their omission from the development process, but has caused the increased impoverishment and subordination of rural women (see, for instance, Rogers, 1980 and Swantz, 1985).

2 *Women's equality is a political, not a developmental issue; a development agency must concern itself with the purely technical matters of increased production and welfare.*

Wrong. The Forward-Looking Strategies make clear that women's development, equality, and empowerment are processes which are intertwined, and women's

development must entail increased control over the factors of production and increased participation in the development process.

3 *Promoting women's equality constitutes undue interference in the Third World country's internal affairs.*

Wrong. For the minority of countries which have not accepted the international convention on women's rights, and which will not accept increased equality for women as being part of their development policies, the development agency should be asking whether any aid programme can be supported in such a country.

The human rights issue seems to be better understood when the problem is discrimination by race. South Africa was an international outcast in the era of apartheid, not merely because there was racial discrimination (this is common in many countries), and not only because racial discrimination was entrenched by law, but mainly because there was no government policy commitment to move in the direction of equality under the law. The same principle should operate in another area of human rights: equality for women.

A respectable multilateral or bilateral development agency should not offer development assistance to a country where women are not equal under the law, and where there is no policy commitment to move towards equality for women. Certainly, the taxpayers who support a bilateral development agency should be able to have the assurance that their money is not being used to support regimes where 'development' causes the increased exploitation and impoverishment of women workers, and where there is no respect for women's rights.

It may well be that the idea that issues of women's rights in any country are purely an internal matter stems from patriarchal attitudes: a belief that women's affairs are a purely domestic issue. According to this line of thinking, how a man treats his wife in his own home is a purely domestic issue; by extension of this thinking, how the ruling male elite treat 'their' women in 'their' country is similarly an internal or domestic issue. If this is the underlying justification for non-interference, then of course it entails a denial that women's equality is a human rights issue, and a belief that male domination is legitimate. In this way, the 'non-interference' argument implicitly denies the human rights principle which lies at the heart of new policies on women's development.

There was a time when the South African government successfully argued that the government's treatment of 'their' blacks was a purely internal matter, in which outsiders should not 'interfere'. But in the area of race relations, such arguments are no longer allowable as a basis for international or bilateral relationships between nations.

4 A development agency must take the existing laws and policies of the Third World country as given, and work within them.

Partly right, but this point has to be kept within its limits, and not over-emphasised or misused. Firstly, policies and laws may be 'given', but they are not fixed. Thus a development agency may agree to work within an existing system of legalised discrimination against women provided that it is clear that there are policies directed towards equality for women, and provided that the development agency is allowed to support projects which contribute to this process towards equality. A country's ratification of the UN Convention already entails a commitment to work towards the removal of legislation and administrative practice which discriminate against women.

Secondly, a development agency should stick to its own policies, and is always in a position to invite the government of a Third World country to adjust its development policies and priorities in the direction of increased women's development in order to attract increased bilateral co-operation.

Thirdly, the development agency may limit its interest to support in particular sectors, or to particular modes of development, where there seems to be a better prospect for women's development.

Fourthly, and as already mentioned above, if the 'given' policies of the Third World government are in complete contradiction to the agency's policies on women's development, then this should be made clear to the Third World government, and no development assistance should be provided until such time as the Third World government can make an acceptable commitment towards women's development.

5 It is not the business of the development agency to seek or promote change in the existing social and customary practices of the Third World country.

Wrong. Where existing social and customary practice stand in the way of development, then it should be among the objectives of the development agency (along with the Third World government) to modify the social practice so that it supports development instead of standing in the way. This is made explicit in the UN Convention which states in its Preamble that the ratifying nations are 'aware that a change in the traditional role of men as well as the role of women in society and in the family is needed to achieve full equality between men and women.'

Countries which have ratified the Convention have also agreed to modify the social and cultural patterns of conduct of men and women, with a view to achieving the elimination of prejudices and customary and all other practices which are based on the idea of the inferiority or the superiority of either of the sexes or on stereotyped roles for men and women. (Article 5a.)

Obviously, there are many aspects of customary rural social practice in the Third World which stand in the way of social and economic development; in women's development the most notable practices retarding development are those which give rural male heads of household exclusive control over land use, labour, and credit, and the distribution of income, even though it is the women who are mostly the farmers and who do most of the agricultural work (see also Longwe, 1988).

Any development project is, by its very nature, a social and economic intervention. A developmental intervention cannot leave traditional social practice untouched, nor ignore the existence of customary practice which stands in the way of development.

6 The development agency's policy on women's development is an attempt to impose Western ideas on women's equality on a Third World country where such ideas are inappropriate.

Wrong. The existence of the UN Convention should make it clear that equality for women is part of a world-wide concern with women's rights, as a major component in the concern with fundamental human rights. Similarly, the existence and general acceptance of the Forward-Looking Strategies shows a world-wide concern with giving women an equal place as participants and beneficiaries in the development process.

The fact that women in Western countries have, in general, a more nearly equal position in society does not mean that such greater freedom should be seen as a purely Western phenomenon, or something which should be confined to the West. It may mean that the struggle by Western women for equality can be a lesson for women of the Third World, and that development agencies can provide a bridge of assistance so that women in the West can assist their more oppressed sisters in the Third World.

It should be realised, too, that although women in the West have taken the lead in the struggle to achieve equality, there are many Western countries where much remains to be done before women achieve an equal place with men. This points to another sense in which the movement for women's equality is part of a worldwide struggle, where women from the West and the Third World can all learn from each other's experience.

7 Women in the Third World are quite content with their position in society, and do not want equality with men.

This, of course, is a variant on the argument that women's equality is a Western concept which should be kept out of the Third World. It may well be true that many women in the Third World, very like their sisters in the West, accept their subordinate position with resignation, and have no thoughts of changing the structure of society. This in itself does not set aside the overall issues of human rights and equal development which have been mentioned above. What it may mean is that the education and conscientisation of women, to enable them to understand their rights and potential, should be a more important part of the development process.

Very often, the claim that 'our women are very content' is made by a member of the male-dominated government bureaucracy that is likely to obstruct women's development. But the claim that women in the Third World are passive and accept their subordinate role needs to be based on the actual empirical evidence of how women think and feel. Obviously if women are very oppressed and suppressed, they are also very silent. Given the opportunity, they may — in my experience — have a lot to say for themselves.

Sara Hlupekile Longwe is a consultant in women's development and an activist for women's rights, based in Zambia. This article is taken from a longer paper, Supporting Women's Development in the Third World: distinguishing between intervention and interference, *which appeared in GADU Newspack 13.*

Fempress: a communication strategy for women

Adriana Santa Cruz

The Latin American Media Network, Fempress, puts out a monthly Latin American magazine, a Press Service on women's issues, and a Radio Press Service covering Latin America.

Fempress was founded in 1981, in Mexico, by two Chilean women living in exile who were passionately convinced that the media are powerful tools to challenge culturally-rooted social injustice. We felt that the people fighting to overturn the legendary culture of *machismo* in Latin America needed a fair and inspirational magazine on every news-stand; one that would reflect the real problems facing women.

Naturally, this was not an immediate possibility. A quick market study exposed the mechanisms by which, even today, it is virtually impossible for alternative media to survive unless it can cover some of its costs by carrying advertisements. Needless to say, advertising acts against women's emancipation almost by definition; and any quest for a profound social change involves swimming against the tide.

As pioneers of this now well-known women's media network, we reached out for international co-operation and trimmed the project down to realistic proportions that excluded the news-stands and the general public but focused instead on strengthening what was then a small and inarticulate Latin American women's movement.

During the 1980s, in the middle of the World Decade for women, solidarity from Northern countries towards Latin America was considerable and the women's movement in the region was in its infancy; there were few Ministries for women's affairs and even fewer with any gender awareness. Women's groups were dispersed, often resenting each other and with virtually no access to the media. There was an evident need to empower and give a voice to all those who were engaged in a cultural change that would make equality possible. Whether working out of universities, churches, institutions, international organisations or governments, women in research, in activism, in politics, and in the media, badly needed to come closer in order to be effective.

Fempress started putting out a modest bulletin, with little more than 200 xeroxed copies, hoping to network throughout the region. That is how the monthly magazine *mujer-fempress* — now printing 5,000 copies — was born. It has been coming out uninterruptedly for 14 years as a unique tool to connect the extremely hetero-geneous movement which women have built for themselves in the Latin American and Caribbean context.

First, from a little office in Mexico City and now, out of what is still a modest space in Santiago, with five full-time workers, Fempress has permanent correspondents writing from Argentina, Bolivia, Brazil, Colombia, Costa Rica, Ecuador, Mexico, Paraguay, Peru, Puerto Rico, Dominican Republic, Uruguay and Venezuela. The correspondents are communicators and feminist activists, with their hearts in the struggle for equality in their own countries.

Today we believe we have achieved many of our goals, although we do not exclusively claim the credit for having brought the different actors working on behalf of women closer than they were in the 1980s. Many factors have contributed, but *mujer-fempress* has played an important role: the magazine is quoted in most bibliographies of research and women's studies, and an average of 15 letters a day reach our offices with the information and the encouragement we need to keep us

going; organisations inform us on the way they xerox Fempress articles for a workshop; documentation centres write on the fact that our magazine is the one most requested; parliamentarians tell us about the way one Fempress article got legislation under way; and indigenous groups let us know they are translating our materials into Aymara in order to reach Peruvian and Bolivian *campesinos* in their own language.

We publish special issues on subjects such as Violence in the Media, Women and Humour, Fears of Women, Population, Black Women, among others. We also produce an annual Portuguese edition of *mujer-fempress* to reach Brazilian readers.

These publications have indeed contributed to communications within the women's movement, but to reach the 'real world' outside we had to look for ways to get articles into the national press, and we have been relatively successful in reaching that goal.

Reaching out through press and radio

Fempress entered the world of mainstream media with the creation of a Press Service, some years after the birth of the journal. However, this had always been a primary goal for us. In the early 1980s, Viviana Erazo, co-founder of Fempress, and myself carried out a study of media and women in Latin America which concluded that media which originate in industrialised countries, such as the cinema, television, and newspapers, and the way in which they are translated or imitated in developing countries, do not reflect the real problems and preoccupations of Third World women.

In our view, if the mass-media did not and still do not provide the information which women need, and insist on presenting an image of the 'ideal woman' which, for ethnic, cultural and economic reasons, is unattainable by the vast majority, it is because there are political and economic interests at stake. In Latin America, as in the United States, women have been moulded to consume goods and hold conservative political views. Women have, in fact, been a force which affirms existing cultural norms and holds back political change in many countries in the region.

' In terms of decision-making, the media is managed mostly by men; and in the editing-rooms of the press and electronic media, women's issues are still considered minor themes, without significant content and with little commercial value. Only recently has this situation begun to change.

In the 1980s, it became evident to Fempress that the capacity — or incapacity — of women to free themselves from the constraints of traditional culture and the trappings of modernity, which cast us all as consumers, depends fundamentally on women's knowledge of the origins of our current situation, and the mechanisms which hold us there. This is why we concentrated our efforts on women's alternative media channels as a means of empowering women through raising awareness and stimulating a process of change.

Fempress does not only aim to increase the flow of alternative information on women's issues in the media, but to create a link between women's groups and the media in order to promote awareness of and a commitment to feminist aims in the media. Getting closer to the mass media means that, through our correspondents, we can identify the newspapers and periodicals which are most sympathetic and willing to publish alternative information about women. Influencing mainstream media is a fundamental factor in generating the cultural change which we seek. Our Press Service is available to all, free of charge; it takes the form of a monthly file with articles and brief notes, covering the material published in the journal. The circulation of this service is rising, and practically all the articles produced for Fempress are reproduced somewhere in the Latin American press. At present, certain articles have appeared in over 20 different media in different countries.

If, at this point, there is any reason to analyse this project, it is because the difficulty in achieving this is well-known to anyone who is promoting 'worthwhile causes'. The United Nations, development agencies or popular movements all know how difficult it is to get their views into the media. 'The media should do this, the media should not do that' are the most repeated prescriptions in any document on development for the past 15 years. Newspaper editing rooms are besieged by the press releases coming from these people, yet few ever occupy a space in their pages. It is in this context that we consider Fempress's achievement.

We believe there are many contributory factors to this relative success: the quality of the information and editorial analysis, the critical but constructive tone, the variety of the issues addressed, the careful selection of correspondents, the quality of personal contacts, and the Latin American character of the service, among others. The articles are written to be of lasting value and rarely based on 'hot' news.

Our press work is strengthened by our links with academics and activists. There have been dozens of seminars and workshops which Fempress has co-organised. In Argentina, Mexico, and Puerto Rico, our correspondents have given courses on non-sexist periodical publishing, at the University and outside. We preach that women must organise more strongly as far as information is concerned: 'it is not enough to do; we must communicate' should be the motto. It is with this conviction that we are soon publishing a manual of non-sexist journalism.

The most significant single reason, however, which explains the relative success of Fempress in getting its articles inside the media, has been its active presence in the women's movement. The influence of the women's movement has spread like an oil spot in recent years; it has fought for supplements and broadsheets on women; it has infiltrated editing rooms, television studios, the radio, and political parties. It is the women's movement which has guaranteed the credibility of the information which Fempress distributes.

In 1993 Fempress identified the need to move into radio, still much more accessible and democratic than television or newspapers. Latin American radio is an ideal channel to reach women who are not involved in the organised women's movement, who are isolated in their homes, working in the field, and who may often be illiterate. More than women in other sectors of the population, these grassroots women need information which makes them feel part of women's struggle for greater equality and recognition.

For this reason, Fempress launched itself into the venture of producing a Radio Information Service for Latin American Women. It comes in the form of a 90-minute cassette, with information, and spoken Fempress articles. This is now being broadcast by 255 radio programmes in the region.

Alternative communications and the market

Finally, we must consider the most critical issue facing women's alternative media work: finance. It is very well-known that international co-operation for development is in crisis; this is particularly true in Latin America, which is not seen as a priority by international development agencies.

However, projects such as Fempress cannot yet finance themselves,[1] and we might further ask whether they will ever be able to do so. Market forces follow the trends of what sells best and, at present,

this seems to be violence, exploitative and abusive sex, and greed for power and consumer goods. Underlying the mainstream media is an agenda which reaffirms the position of those who hold power and hardly allows the possibility of change based on alternative values. The mass media, which are the principal power within societies which call themselves democratic, are integrally financed by advertising. A serious debate on these issues is tragically missing.

In this situation, what happens to ideas which are not in line with those of the people who hold economic power? What tools can we use to promote humane societies when we are surrounded by all that is dehumanising, if we cannot rely on media which do not depend exclusively on advertising and profit-oriented values? Without funds, how can we broaden the thinking capacity of a society, and strengthen the people who question the ways in which our societies are run?

A fundamental element of the alternative communication media should be to help to correct and compensate for the market's shortcomings, which are many and serious.

Public policy-makers, and those who are battling for social development with equity for women and men, look to international co-operation to provide inspiration, mutual support, and funding, to affect change. It is important to value and recognise the importance of such non-governmental projects which, like this one, have been possible thanks to international co-operation. National and international media networks have helped to raise awareness of women's struggle, to communicate good ideas, inspire govern-ments, and strengthen civil society. Their failure to survive might leave us all even more stranded in these deeply distressing times.

1. Its budget is close to US$400,000 a year and its funders are: Sida, Sweden; Cida, Canada; Norad, Norway; The Ford Foundation, USA; UNIFEM, United Nations; UNFPA, United Nations; The Federation Genevoise de Cooperation, Switzerland; and The Ministry of Foreign Affairs, The Netherlands

INTERVIEW

'I, Black Woman, Resist!'

Katrina Payne talks to Alzira Rufino

Alzira Rufino, feminist and activist, founded the Casa de Cultura da Mulher Negra, the Black Women's House of Culture, which was the first black women's centre in Brazil. The centre was opened in the city of Santos in 1990 and is run by the Black Women's Collective of Baixada Santista, with funding support from War on Want. It offers legal support for the survivors of racism, and domestic and sexual violence, and works to empower black women and raise community awareness of discrimination against women and black people. The centre runs a variety of cultural activities, from popular education and training, to a newspaper and a black people's art gallery.

How did you first become politically active?
I have always been very interested in politics and motivated by it. My father and my grandfather were involved in politics so I think it is in my blood! My interest started in school and in college and I knew that I was black and a woman, and in a country with so many problems. I saw that the black women were in the lowest-paid jobs with no access to education or training and I knew that black women needed to press the authorities and the government for public policies that could benefit them. I also thought that black women should denounce society's racism, because I am sure that no child is born racist; it is society and the media that makes him or her racist.

Why did you decide to create the Case de Cultura da Mulher Negra?
I decided to create the centre because Santos is a very sexist and racist city. Santos is the main port in Brazil, and in the whole of South America, and there's a lot of violence due to the port. Women are the majority of the population in Santos and this is where we now have our centre. The centre was created by black women and we offer assistance to women, both black and white.

What gave you the idea?
It was when I was working to promote the first ever united celebration of International Women's Day in the region, back in 1985, that the idea started to form. For the first time, small groups of women gathered together to celebrate 8 March in Santos. But during the mobilisation for the International Day, I felt that black women's participation was lacking, we were too few and we were too silent. I saw that nobody else was working on women's and black rights, so I formed a black women's group, the Colectivo de Mulheres Negras da Baixada Santista.

Why did you decide to name the centre The House of Culture?

As black women have historically been the main preservers of family survival and African tradition, I think that the African roots of black women and black people should be preserved and promoted, which is what we do in our centre. Our culture is shown in every aspect of our centre. We have African decorations and furniture, typical Afro-Brazilian food, African clothes for sale, and cultural activities like *capoeira*. We also have a children's choir 'Omo Oya' to rescue the Yoruba songs and rhythms of the African heritage in Brazil.

I am also a priest of the Afro-Brazilian religion Candomblé. According to my religion I have as my two main protectors Oxum and Aia, two female gods. It is my role to help to rescue and preserve this cultural and religious tradition.

How important is culture for black women in Brazil?

Our culture and religious tradition is very important because we have the female gods which are so dominant in Candomblé. Women are more important than men in Candomblé. It is black women who perform the main functions and this helps to raise their self-esteem. By promoting and preserving the many contributions of African culture, we show the importance and value of African roots, and this helps black women to value themselves.

In the centre we try to strengthen black aesthetics by showing that black women's hair and racial traits are beautiful and that African clothes are lovely, so we counter the tendency for women to 'whiten' themselves, with this strengthening of African traditions, and aspects of culture and self-image.

LARRY BOYD/OXFAM

Children learning capoeira, a traditional dance form based on ritualised kick–boxing, part of the black African cultural heritage of Brazil.

So what would you say is the dominant culture in Brazil?

White men dominate the culture, along with the white race, but it is mainly white men. Although black people make the culture, with samba, Carnival, Afro-Brazilian dances and rhythms. The ones who make the money from our culture are the white men.

With Carnival, for example, tradition-ally it was the older black women who were always involved. And we still are, we make the clothes and the decorations and we actively participate. We black women organise a parade and hold events to raise funds for it.

The black girls and younger women are also actively involved. They are usually at the front of the parade, where these beautiful young women are the main focus of the media who highlight their bodies and their sensuality in a sexual way. But after three days of amusement they go back to their jobs as maids and cleaners, where they are poorly paid and don't have any rights. These young women are the main targets for sexual harassment and they are also led into prostitution by white men and tourists.

Unfortunately black women and black men are no longer in charge of the samba schools. Black people used to control this great show that is Carnival but now it's a source of huge income, and the over-whelming majority of the presidents of the samba schools are white men. A lot of them are involved in gambling. Talking of Carnival, this reminds me of a song by a popular singer in Brazil, Leci Brandao. I like this song very much, he sings of black people being such good dancers and such good footballers, but he asks when will we be sitting at the decision-makers' table.

Did you have any criticism when you opened the centre?

Yes we did! The first criticism was because it was a women's centre, and it was the first in the region, and the second was because it was a black women's centre, and it was the first in Brazil. It would have been more acceptable to the community to have a black centre, for men and women. So there has been a lot of criticism due to it being a women's, and mainly a black women's, centre.

Yet I think it was necessary to be so specific. It was important to have a black women's centre because black men don't understand the needs of black women as women, and the feminist movement in Brazil didn't understand that, although black women have common issues as women, they have specific concerns as black women.

Does the feminist movement recognise black women's issues now?

After many years of work, almost a decade, and with the creation of black women's groups, now the feminist movement is beginning to take the specific issues of black women into consideration. And, for their part, black women activists have decided to leave the back of the stage and to stop being secondary actors. We are taking the main roles, because if half the Brazilian population is black and women are 52 per cent of the population, we are aware that we are half the female population in Brazil.

As black women we want to rescue our history and our participation in the women's movement and the black move-ment. After the abolition of slavery, black women were the main means of the family's survival. Black women were the first feminists in Brazil. Since the abolition of slavery, black women were econom-ically independent of men. They used to sell food and sweets which they had made themselves, and work as maids and cooks. They raised their children, and supported their male partners, because the men couldn't find jobs.

But don't some women feel that consciousness-raising and culture is irrelevant if they are still living in poverty?

I think that through culture we can bring the revolution! The first step is to increase women's awareness of their racial identity. This increases black women's self-esteem and can lead to women being trained for better jobs. The next step is to stimulate the black woman and man so that they can take the initiative to make their own money through their own skills and culture, not by working for somebody else but by having their own businesses. For example, in our country, black women are thought to be the best cooks, but usually they work in white homes for a very low wage. Well, we can encourage them to open their own catering businesses, for example, and be their own boss. And similarly with music. We are encouraging black women to earn money from their own skills. We have encouraged black handicraft co-operatives, and these artisans are now living from their craft and arts.

As a model of what I am saying, our centre has a restaurant which serves typical Afro-Brazilian food, which is open to everyone. But they have to pay a high price because they are not going to a normal restaurant, they are coming to a cultural centre, so they must support the centre's activities and pay a bit more for this! We have a lot of customers, because the food is good.

Are you optimistic about the future for black women in Brazil?

Yes I am. Black women are advancing and occupying some of the positions that were denied us before. Black women are 'coming out' and denouncing on an international stage the racism and the sexism they experience in Brazil.

Family group, Recife, Brazil.

COLIN PEARSON/OXFAM

Resources

Color, Class and Country: Experiences of Gender

Gay Young and Bette Dickerson (eds)
Zed Books, 1994.

Those of us who have a European Caucasian identity may never have the opportunity to reflect in the way that Kathryn Ward has done during her own intellectual and political journey, on race and gender, but her paper 'How scholarship by and about women of colour shaped my life as a white feminist' could well be a starting point.

Her paper comes near the end of this volume by social scientists. All the studies discuss aspects of what the authors describe as 'the intersections of gender, class and race', some dealing with two of these aspects, while Bette Dickerson, Ward's co-editor, in her own article, deals with all three.

An international perspective is evident with studies referring to a variety of countries including Turkey, Chile and Mexico, as well as an ambitiously titled paper 'Gender inequality around the world; comparing fifteen nations in five world regions', written by Gay Young (co-editor) and others. The overall impression

is a well-researched critique of the US feminist discourse. Ward, Dickerson and Samarasinghe have rethought this essentially white middle-class feminist discourse, and, in discussing the black feminist perspective, plead that it sit at the centre of the feminist debate and not at its periphery. Although I applaud this stance, I do have difficulty with the preoccupation with the white middle-class feminist debate in its entirety, on the grounds that this may appeal to the US market, but not necessarily reflect the views or needs of feminists or gender and development workers in Bangladesh or Ethiopia.

It seems inevitable that with an ambitious volume such as this, use of social science jargon will hinder the reader, so it was with some relief that I encountered definitions given by Bette Dickerson (as late as Chapter 6) of such terms as ethnicity, feminism, black feminism, and community. The relief was necessary after encountering such terms as 'displaced homemaker', 'women of colour', and 'racial common fate identification' (which Dickerson herself used and defines)! One cannot help but note how much lengthier the sentences are when the authors are endeavouring to incorporate so many aspects of political correctness.

In their articles, Wendy Luttrell and Mary Romero discuss women's aspirations and opportunities. In her study of urban white working class women, and Southern rural black women, Luttrell shows how young girls' hopes and dreams may be far removed from the reality of their later lives. In one of a group of articles centering on women and economic issues, Romero's research centres on domestic workers' aspirations to the status of 'housekeeper', rather than 'maid', deftly negotiating the employee — employer relationship so that the household tasks and not personal ones were performed.

Stan Gray's paper, on a Canadian court case concerning sexual harassment of a female employee of a large steel corporation, shows how the issues of race and gender are linked in complex ways to that of employment in the 1990s: 'As the recession takes its ever more devastating toll, employers and government try to divide workers against each other. They encourage the scape-goating of women and of people of other races, regions, colours, and countries. In the face of all this, it is ever more important to stress what unites us while respecting these differences.'

In its survey of women and economics, this volume highlights Structural Adjustment Programmes (SAPs). 'What do women do when there aren't enough hours in a day?' asks Maria Floro in the title of her study. She found that expenditure adjustments within the household in the light of SAPs usually 'require more input of women's unpaid labour both in terms of preparation and shopping/marketing', that is, 'the need to find the cheapest sources and to buy smaller quantities more often'. Christine Obbo in her graphic description of Uganda before and after the Amin regime describes SAPs as being the supposed cure for economic decline whereas the reality is of women and children bearing the brunt of "the IMF's Structural Adjustment Programmes".

Obbo assesses how women's economic disadvantage has been addressed by Women in Development (WID) policies;

she believes that the low wages, low prices for crops and reduced government expenditures have added greatly to women's poverty and therefore their vulnerability. Obbo asserts that development has not only passed poor Ugandan women by, but that their interests are not adequately represented by elite women working in development, who have the opportunity to speak on behalf of the poor, and do so in a foreign language — namely English.

Elizabeth Fox-Genovese, a feminist theorist, neatly shows how the Women's Movement must reflect upon its own agenda and summarises where it should be going. She believes that it is at a crossroads in that 'difference has replaced equality as a central concern of feminist theory', and asks us to consider 'thinking differently about difference'. Although the Women's Movement exists because women share certain 'characteristics which differentiate them from men', Fox-Genovese rightly stresses that the 'vitality of a women's movement in our time depends upon the recognition that women are also divided by class and race.'

Any reader who is familiar with the writings of bel hooks or Angela Davis will identify with Kathryn Ward's conclusion that 'white women need to be silent for a spell, while they read, study and listen to women of colour'. When the reader reaches her or his own conclusions, the desire to be silent, and to read, study and listen will probably prevail.

Review by Janette Davies, a Research Associate at the Centre for Cross-Cultural Research on Women, in the University of Oxford.

Organisations working on culture

Women in Black: a network of women who oppose militarism, violence, and enforced ethnic separation; activities in many countries including Israel, Argentina, former Yugoslavia, Brazil, Philippines, Germany, India, and the Netherlands. Women in Black, Dragoslava Papovica br 9/10, 11000 Belgrade, SERBIA. Tel/fax: 38 11 334 706.

Committee of Women Religious Against Trafficking in Women: international network aiming to draw attention to trafficking in women and to support and stimulate local organisations to offer help to returning victims. PO Box 104, 2120 AB Bennebroek, The Netherlands.

Women Living Under Muslim Laws: formed in 1984, a network of women whose lives are shaped, conditioned or governed by laws, both written and unwritten, drawn from interpretations of the Koran tied up with local traditions. Provides and disseminates information for women and women's groups in Muslim communities, supports women's struggles within Muslim countries and publicises these outside, and provides channel of communication. Produces publications and newsletters. Main office: Boite Postale 23, 34790 Grabels, France. Asia Office: 38/8 Sarwar Road, Lahore Cantt., Pakistan.

Women Against Fundamentalism: founded in 1989 to challenge the rise of fundamentalism in all religions. Focuses on Britain and beyond. Defends individual women and women's organisations against fundamentalist attacks; supports non-religiously based refuges and protection for women experiencing violence inside and outside the home; disseminates information within Britain and outside; researches and studies the common strands of fundamentalism in all religions; fosters international links and works in solidarity with similar movements in other countries. 129 Seven Sisters Road, London N7 7QG, tel. 0171 272 6563, fax 0171 272 5476.

Mothers in Action, Kenya: assists and supports Kenyan women and children in violent and abusive situations. Provides support and legal advice. Po Box 54562 Nairobi, Kenya, tel. 443868/440299

The Musasa Project, Zimbabwe: public education on gender violence; counselling; training on counselling; publications production. 133 Rotten Row, Harare, Zimbabwe, tel. 794983.

Southall Black Sisters, UK: founded in 1979 to meet the needs of Asian and Afro–Caribbean women living in the UK. Supports and counsels women facing violence and abuse at home. Campaigns to bring about change in the social, political, economic and cultural constrictions on women's freedom. 52 Norwood Road, Southall, Middlesex, UK. Tel. 0181 571 9595, fax. 081 574 6787.

Further reading

Culture

Ann Oakley, *Sex, Gender and Society*, revised 1985, Temple Smith/Gower. Originally written in 1971, this classic book draws on cross-cultural studies to emphasise that, rather than being 'natural', gender identities are a social construct.

Valentine M Moghadam (ed) *Identity Politics and Women: Cultural Reassertions and Feminisms in Perspective* Westview Press, 1994. This book considers the rise of political and cultural movements which are bidding for political power, legal changes or cultural supremacy, basing their claims on notions of religious, ethnic or national identity. From examining such movements' attitudes to women, and attempts to control female freedom and sexuality through invoking Woman as a cultural symbol, the book moves to assess women's own response. Uses 13 case studies from Muslim, Christian, Jewish and Hindu societies.

Violence against women

Jill Taylor and Sheelagh Stewart, *Sexual and Domestic Violence: Help, Recovery and Action in Zimbabwe*, Women and Law in Southern Africa, PO Box UA 171, Union Avenue, Harare, Zimbabwe, 1991.

Lori L Heise, *Overcoming Violence: A Background Paper on Violence Against Women as an Obstacle to Development*, paper produced for Oxfam's Women's Linking Project, 1993, available from the Gender Team, Oxfam UK

Margaret Schuler, ed., *Freedom from Violence: Women's Strategies From Around the World*, 1992, UNIFEM

Conflict

Judy El Bushra and Eugenia Piza Lopez, *Development in Conflict: the Gender Dimension*, Oxfam Publications, Oxford, 1994, (also available free of charge to Southern organisations who lack funds, on application to the Gender Team, Oxfam UK).

Periodicals

There are many national and international journals worldwide which are committed to using the media as a tool to promote gender equity. Here is only a short selection of these:

Agenda: a South African journal about women and gender, published bi–monthly. Agenda Collective, 29 Ecumenical Centre Trust, 20 St Andrews Street, Durban, 4001, South Africa. Tel. 031 3054074, fax 031 3016611

Arise: a Ugandan women's development magazine published by ACFODE (Action for Development). Quarterly. Acfode House, Bukoto, PO Box 6729, Kampala, Uganda. Tel/fax: 532311.

Everywoman: Britain's only national feminist magazine, offering an alternative to mainstream media. Everywoman, 34 Islington Green, London N1 8DU, UK. Tel: 071 359 5496, fax: 071 226 9448.

Laya: quarterly women's development journal from the Philippines, published by Laya Women's Collective, 35 Scout Delgado Street,Quezon City, Philippines. Tel: 998034.

Mujer/Fempress: Latin American women's journal, published by Fempress, ILET Casilla 16–637, Correo 9/Santiago, Chile, tel. 231 5486.